ECO-THEOLOGY

TOWARD A RELIGION
FOR OUR TIMES

ECO-THEOLOGY

TOWARD A RELIGION
FOR OUR TIMES

HENRYK SKOLIMOWSKI

CREATIVE FIRE PRESS
- 2020 -

First published by Vasanta Press: Adyar, Madras, India (1985). This edition includes supplemental material from A Sacred Place to Dwell (1994), Dharma, Ecology, & Wisdom (1999), and Let There Be Light (2010).

Edited by David Skrbina.

Library of Congress Cataloging-in-Publication Data

Skolimowski, Henryk (1930-2018)
Eco-Theology: Toward a Religion for Our Times

p. cm.

Includes bibliographical references and index.

ISBN 978-1734-8042-32
(pbk.: alk. paper)
1. Philosophy of religion 2. Environmental philosophy

Printing number: 9 8 7 6 5 4 3 2 1

Printed in the United States of America on acid-free paper.

TABLE OF CONTENTS

FOREWORD

David Skrbina, PhD

When Henryk Skolimowski died in April of 2018, he left behind a monumental legacy of creativity, inspiration, and philosophical innovation. Unconstrained by philosophical dogma, and open to all new ideas and new possibilities, he broke new ground in a number of areas of philosophy. His early work in the philosophy of technology established him as a prominent and prescient critic of the technological phenomenon—something which grows more relevant by the day. His invention of eco-philosophy was among the first serious efforts to merge philosophy and environmentalism in a meaningful way, and to spell out the consequences for society. And his courage to do philosophy in a theological vein, and to employ religious concepts and ideas, cut against the grain of the secular materialism that was (and is) prominent in the Western world.

By the early 1970s, and inspired by the likes of Schweitzer and Teilhard, Skolimowski had begun to weave religious themes into his work. Already in 1974, he was speaking of "reverence for nature," and of the world as "a sanctuary"—concepts with distinctly theological underpinnings. In 1976, his thesis of "ecological humanism" invoked the ideas of faith, worship, transcendence, and the divine in a philosophical context. Here, evolution assumes supreme importance; it is the lens by which all phenomena and all philosophy must be filtered. Evolution—conceived as a cosmic process of 'order out of chaos,' and not merely something biological—brought forth stars, planets, life, and humans. It then brought forth ideas, concepts, symbols, and civilization. Soon enough, it brought forth the notions of gods, spirits, and the divine. In conceiving such things, said Skolimowski, we make them real. Therefore, evolution is, rightly seen, a process of *divinization*—of creating spirituality, the divine, and even God. The evolutionary path of the cosmos is a path on the way to God: to the most luminous, the most divine, the most spiritual. As leading lights in evolution (at least here on Earth), we humans participate deeply in this cosmic process.

In his path-breaking work of 1981, *Eco-Philosophy*, Skolimowski elaborated on the necessity and value of such religious thinking:

> If you worship nothing, you are nothing. ... [T]he primary function of religious structures is to provide a framework for ideals which are inspiring and sustaining to our life. ... Religion transforms reality, with a view to making man unselfish and altruistic; it inspires him to live within the human family and help to reconcile man with himself. ...

Religion, ultimately, is an instrument in man's search for his identity, his integrity—in his painful struggles with himself to attain and preserve his humanity and spirituality.

[T]he cosmos is pervaded with spirituality, which leads to the realization that we are a part of a sacred tapestry. We shall need to create a new theology, for no worldview is complete without a theology... The new theology underlying Ecological Humanism is that we are God-in-the-process-of-becoming. We are fragments of grace and spirituality *in status nascendi* [in the process of being born]. We give testimony to our extraordinary divine potential by actualizing these fragments in us. ... This *ecological theology* provides not only a new cosmological scheme; it also has an existential import... (pp. 108-115)

Here we have the outlines of his "ecological theology"—that is, of Eco-theology.

From even these short excerpts, we see that Skolimowski's use of words is unique. When he speaks of *religion, theology, God, spirit,* or *heaven,* for example, he is thinking in very different terms than usual. For him, 'religion' deals with ultimate human goals and purposes—the 'why' of our existence. 'God' is not someone dwelling in heaven, not a guy in a big white beard to whom we pray. Rather, God is a measure of our ultimate being; it is a "realization of our spiritual nature"; a symbol of the ultimate wholeness and oneness of the universe. 'Spirit' is not some immortal, ghostly soul, but rather the human essence, our truest and deepest human nature. 'Heaven' is not a supernatural realm but rather a recognition of the greatness and perfection toward which all the cosmos is evolving. All these traditional concepts need to be reconceived, he said, in light of evolution and advances in physics.

Eco-theology, then, is a thoroughly *naturalistic* phenomenon—indeed, it is the most natural thing in the world: to respect and revere that process of nature by which we came into existence on this vibrant planet Earth. In Eco-theology, God is an ideal of perfection, not some supernatural being. There is no traditional heaven, no traditional hell; these are mere fables from a bygone era. The entire question of the afterlife is, in fact, left completely open—as befitting a topic of which can know nothing. Importantly, in Eco-theology there are no divine saviors who have come to Earth to "save" humanity; we must save ourselves, insists Skolimowski. There is no one else. The burden of responsibility falls squarely on our shoulders. We must act, here and now, to save our planet and to realize the best possible life for all humanity. Have reverence toward nature, see the world as a sanctuary, and view yourself, and all people, as sparks of divinity on the path to greatness and light. This, in a nutshell, is Eco-theology.

The following text is derived primarily from Skolimowski's 1985 booklet, *Eco-Theology*. This small work, however, suffered from a number of technical shortcomings. It was published in Madras, India by a small theosophical press (Vasanta) which had no real distribution network to speak of. Furthermore, the well-intended publishers were perhaps less capable of such matters as careful editing in the English language, and hence the original displayed a considerable number of typographical errors and linguistic confusions. Owing to a lack of distribution, the booklet was never easily obtained, and thus had little circulation. All these shortcomings have been alleviated with the current reissue.

Skolimowski, of course, continued to write on eco-theological matters well after his initial 1985 booklet. In order to supplement the original writings, included here are relevant portions from some of his later works, including material from (now out of print) books like *A Sacred Place to Dwell* (1994) and *Dharma, Ecology, and Wisdom* (1999). Also included is a lengthy chapter from one of Skolimowski's last major works, *Let There Be Light* (2010). These supplemental writings help to flesh out and articulate his conception of a truly inspiring Eco-theology: of a religious vision that meets the urgent needs of the present day.

With a bit of luck, and with the blessings of the gods, this new book will take us a few more steps along the road to salvation.

David Skrbina, editor
1 June 2020

PREAMBLE

IF RELIGION is about wholeness, what is the structure of wholeness appropriate for our times? Why is traditional religion, and specifically traditional Christianity, failing us? If the announcement of the death of God is premature, what kind of new images of God must we evolve so that religion once more becomes a life-enhancing phenomenon? If we cannot live with traditional God, and we cannot live without God, what kind of God should we aim at to replace traditional, and by and large obsolete, notions of God? What is the nature of our spirituality, and in which ways is it indispensable to our well-being? If evolution can be seen as a spiritual process—in addition to being a biological one—to what degree can we identify the process of divination with the characteristics of evolution unfolding? In what sense can we talk about *evolutionary* God?

What is the new sense of grace, and of responsibility, within the evolutionary framework? To what degree has traditional (Newtonian) science undermined our quest for spirituality? In which sense is the New Physics encouraging us to take spirituality, and the religious quest, seriously? To what degree does our image of God—and the religious structure that goes with this image—determine the nature of reality surrounding us? And vice versa: to what degree does our current notion of reality determine the nature of our God? If Eco-philosophy is taken seriously as providing a new *Weltanschauung*, a new worldview, to what degree can it help us to construct Eco-theology? How can we fuse ecology—conceived as a metaphor for inter-connectedness and inter-relatedness of all living things—with theology—conceived as an abode for refining our spirituality and a focus of reflection concerning man's ultimate destiny? How can ecology and Christianity be fused together? What are the implications of seeing all religions as manifestations of the Big Light of the cosmos?

These questions will be explored in the book that follows. In the 21st century, too much of our energy and time has been spent on attending trivia. It is time that we start a discussion on things fundamental. Mankind's essential nature is not defined by his trivial pursuits but by those sublime questions which bring him closer to heaven.

Eco-Theology in Relation to Eco-Cosmology

Eco-theology is a part of an over-arching scheme that we may call Eco-Cosmology. The latter has at least three branches: 1) Eco-Theology, the subject of this book. 2) Eco-Praxis: this has been most visible since the advent of the Ecology Movement in the 1970s. Soft Technology, or Alternative Technology, or Appropriate Technology, are all aspects of Eco-Praxis. 3) Eco-Philosophy, which has been articulated in four different directions, respectively by myself,[1] Arne Naess, Thomas Berry, and the Deep Ecology movement. There is a considerable overlapping among the four and some disagreements.

Eco-Theology is still in its infancy. It will have to be articulated and incorporated into our ecological lifestyles—if we are to make these lifestyles coherent and justified in depth. Action without reflection is blind; reflection without action is impotent—to echo Immanuel Kant. We need to sort out the deeper questions before we can go on with our Eco-Praxis. Eco-Philosophy and Eco-Theology are fundamental because they provide the rationale for our actions, and also make sense of our existence. A regeneration of our individual lifestyles will not be possible, and bringing about equity and justice to the human family extremely difficult, unless we attend to the deepest questions that characterize our existence. These questions are religious in nature.

Religion is not an opiate for the masses, it is part of the scaffolding of our being. When we attempt to give it the ultimate justification, ethics merges with religion. This is also true of our basic concepts of daily praxis. For the mind which is forever watchful and supremely aware of the mystery of existence, the mundane contains some aspects of the divine, and the divine can be seen in the manifestations of the mundane.

---

[1] See my books *Eco-Philosophy: Designing New Tactics for Living* (1981) and *Living Philosophy: Eco-Philosophy as a Tree of Life* (1992).

CHAPTER 1

WHY DO WE RETURN TO RELIGION?

WHY DO we return to religion? We have got plenty of answers from physics and chemistry, from psychology and immunology, from philosophy and sociology. Yet important questions remain unsolved: What is the meaning of our life? What is our destiny? What is the structure of our wholeness? And how can it be justified in human terms? And in terms that go beyond the human universe? How can we cope with the mystery of existence? How should we contemplate death and the possibility of life after death? What has created us and to what purpose?

Those sublime questions go beyond all specialized disciplines. Unless we resolve such questions, we cannot claim to be fully human. Traditional religions have lost their visions; their creative substance is exhausted. For this reason, many turn a deaf ear at the very sound of 'religion' as the term signifies for them a petrified structure—a form of existence that is tantamount to impoverishment, the process of being dragged down rather than being elevated. Yet whatever your attitude toward traditional religion, the sublime questions must be contemplated by anybody who seeks enlightenment. These questions are religious in nature. Even if one wishes to dissociate oneself completely from traditional religion, and from traditional concepts of deity, one has to acknowledge the religious sense of life for, without it, life is singularly empty. We have lost the religious sense of life within which the ultimate meaning resides.

E. F. Schumacher's *Small is Beautiful* is a seminal statement of the 1970s. Yet this book does not express the ultimate Schumacher. During the last years of his life he called for a 'metaphysical reconstruction.' In his opinion, Western civilization, and especially the technological society, has been on a mistaken course. This course is based on a metaphysical error, or a philosophical error: we have conceived wrongly what is most important in life. This misconception is of a religious nature, for it involves the ultimate human concerns which are not tackled by any specialized disciplines—save religion and theology.

When the time came for Schumacher to provide his metaphysical reconstruction, he produced the book entitled *A Guide for the Perplexed* (1977), which is a religious treatise. Although deep in many ways, and shining through with wonderful insights, this book is ultimately disappointing. For the *Guide* is a restatement of Catholic theology, conceived and executed in the frame of reference of Thomas Aquinas. The treatise is disappointing because many expected from Schumacher a religious statement for our times, uniquely expressing our dilemmas. Thus many had expected of Schumacher to provide an outline of Eco-theology. With his supreme grasp of the interconnectedness of all forms of life within the ecosystem, with his exquisite sensitivities and deep religious convictions, he was almost predestined to be a religious spokesperson for the ecological era. This did not happen. *A Guide for the Perplexed* is an expression of the theology of yesteryear rather than a theology for our times.

Schumacher was a saintly man endowed with a great deal of wisdom which emanated from him on various occasions. Yet the *Guide* suffers the symptoms of overzealousness. We needed more than a restatement of Thomas Aquinas. Christianity, to be a vital and transforming force again, must first revitalize and transform itself. This may also be said of other traditional religions.

Great transformational changes are sweeping the world—transforming cultures and our consciousness in their wake. They require an in-depth response on the level of our religious consciousness. The core of our beliefs has changed. We can no longer believe in the simple story of creation as presented in the Bible. For we have in front of our eyes the evidence of the convulsing becoming of the universe over the last 15 billion years. We can no longer believe in a static, immutable, and frozen God. For we know that its conception was an invention of ancient people who lived simply and created their God in the image of their simple and seemingly immutable world. We can no longer believe in the Paradise Lost, for the evolutionary perspective informs us that we are on a continuous spiral, and that therefore there never was a Paradise, and none was lost; except in our myths.

On the other hand, we can no longer believe that God is dead. We no longer believe in the arrogance of secular humanism. We no longer believe in pipe dreams of narrow-minded scientists and technologists who have promised us salvation through material gratification.

God is alive for us, for we are alive as spiritual beings. God for us is the recognition and realization of our spiritual nature. We are alive, but often cracked, and sometimes mutilated. The specific *religious needs* of our times must be related to our wholeness, to the process of healing of our fractured existence.

The question of wholeness is one related to the meaning of life, and what we are here for. The ultimate concerns require the ultimate frame of reference—which is religion. Thus, when one finds oneself in a situation in which no further recourse to any other evidence is available but one's 'innermost beliefs,' 'innermost convictions,'—then one acts on the basic of a *religious attitude*, even if one shies away from the term 'religion.'

Religion for our times must first make the individual whole within, before he or she can be made one with the Great Whole outside. Indeed, we have come to understand that the more the individual is whole within himself or herself, the more he/she becomes at one with the Great Whole. This is one of the new principles of understanding ourselves in religious terms.

CHAPTER 2

THE FOUR STAGES OF EVOLUTION

IN WHAT SENSE can we talk about evolutionary God? If evolution applies to all there is, then it applies to our *thinking* about religion and God.

As we think, so we become. As we become, so we think. The process of our becoming spells out different modes of thinking about religion and God. Traditional religions attempt to bring us back to a context which we have outgrown. They impose on us old language and old metaphors which were suitable for former times. Therefore, not only must we find different religious contexts—appropriate for our religious needs—but also different ways of *thinking* about religion, about God, about our spiritual heritage.

A terminological note: When I speak of evolution, I do not merely mean the Darwinian kind of evolution; even less so do I mean Social Darwinism—which is a form of ideology, supporting injustice and inequity. In short, I do not mean any deterministic process which, for example, Jacques Monod postulates in his book *Chance and Necessity*, that makes us victims of iron necessity and/or capricious chance.

I use the term 'evolution' in the sense in which Bergson and Teilhard applied it, as a partly creative process which alone can account for emergent qualities and new forms of life. All *significant* changes in the history of the universe are the result of evolution so conceived; 'significant' invariably means within the compass of our understanding. Thus evolution is inextricably tied to our understanding of the development of the universe, and our understanding of our place in it.

Everything evolves. So does our thinking about evolution. It has evolved significantly since Charles Darwin came on the stage. As it was important in Darwin's times to see the unity of mankind with lower forms of life, so it is important in our times to see the differences between human beings and lower forms of life. Evolution means differentiation; it means growing complexity and growing consciousness. Whoever is blind to those characteristics of evolution is blind to the very *raison d'etre* of evolution.

Let us therefore attempt to see how our thinking about evolution has evolved, and how it is evolving now. Insofar as we are evolution conscious of itself, we have the responsibility to help this process of evolving.

To begin with, the discovery of evolution does not start with Darwin but with the geologist Charles Lyell. Lyell saw and described the geological evolution in his seminal treatise *Principles of Geology* (1830-33). By the time Darwin came onto the stage, the ground was prepared. People were ready to entertain ideas about evolution.

Their imagination could *conceive* that the world was evolving. Darwin applied Lyell's idea a step further and showed that species were evolving as well. Thus we witness the first two stages in the discovery of evolution:

1. Geological (Lyell)
2. Biological (Darwin)

The next two stages of this discovery are happening under our very eyes. We are actually articulating them, sometimes consciously and sometimes only gropingly. These next two stages in our discovery of evolution are the recognition of *conceptual* evolution, and then of *theological* evolution—which, because of the nature of traditional religions, is most difficult for people to accept.

3. Conceptual
4. Theological

The recognition of conceptual evolution (3) is based on the realization that all our knowledge is evolving, that our mind and our knowledge are not fixed forms— once and for all. Put otherwise: there are no absolute laws of science which ultimately describe physical reality. All knowledge is conjectural (Karl Popper). The New Physics goes a step further: the known and the knower merge. As our minds evolve, so will our knowledge, as well as our 'laws' of science. ('The nature of the laws of nature changes,' to paraphrase Prigogine). A recognition of the fallibility of all human knowledge, including scientific knowledge, was just an extension of the evolutionary perspective into the realm of knowledge and of conceptual thinking. The lion's share of credit in this respect goes to Karl Popper who, in his *Conjectures and Refutations* (1963), tirelessly argued that fixed scientific laws is an illusion. We only have conjectures, tenuous and tentative, holding only for a while, and then they are replaced by other conjectures. It should be noted that Popper himself did not perceive that his epistemology was an extension of evolutionary theory into the products of our knowledge. This interpretation has become possible only with the advent of the New Physics. The New Physics, as I will argue, exemplifies the third stage of our evolutionary thinking: evolutionary thinking applied to thinking itself; seeing our minds as a part of the evolutionary process.

The recognition of theological evolution (4), or the discovery of evolution in the realm of our thinking about God and theology, means that we no longer accept one fixed and immutable God. We thus recognize that our concept of deity, of redemption, of salvation are evolutionary products too. We shall need to spell out this insight in some detail. As evolution goes on, our being changes. As we change, our minds change. As our minds change, our deities change, our thinking about ultimate concerns and ultimate anchors change. Eco-theology, as well as creation theology, represents the fourth stage in the discovery of evolution.

CHAPTER 2

The two latter stages in the discovery of evolution—the conceptual and the theological—are so close to us that we do not have a sufficient perspective to see them clearly. To sharpen our perception of these stages, I shall discuss the old physics and the old theology vis a vis the New Physics and the New Theology. Let me emphasize one point as a prelude: In the old frame of reference, all is fixed, the whole world is viewed as one static frame of a film. The new frame of reference (stages 3 and 4) means that the film is *running*, that viewing it as one static frame was just the result of a limited vision.

CHAPTER 3

ECO-THEOLOGY VIS A VIS
THE NEW PHYSICS

THEOLOGY and physics are vastly different subjects. Yet on some level of discourse they interconnect. They interconnect on the level of ultimate assumptions of a given cosmology. As shocking as it may appear to some, I shall suggest that Newtonian physics was a form of codification of the basic tenets of the Judeo-Christian Theology. Newton wanted to re-establish the glory of God; a perfect God could not have created an imperfect disharmonious universe. Showing that all phenomena in heaven and on earth obey the same immutable set of laws was a demonstration of the perfection of God— through the harmony of His creation. Let us be supremely aware that it was the Christian God that inspired Newton's design. The biblical story of Genesis subconsciously guided Newton's conception of the physical universe.

Newtonian Physics is in the image of Jehovah of the Old Testament. Protestant Ethics is an extension of both. The three of them—the theology of the Old Testament, Newtonian Physics, and the Protestant

Ethic—spell out our essential unfreedom. We are crushed on three sides: by the will of the inscrutable God, by the deterministic laws of physics, by the paralyzing grip of morality according to which you slave and slave and slave here on earth, and your rewards ... may be in heaven.

This essential enslavement ends with the New Physics and the New Theology, each of which sheds a new light not only on the nature of the physical reality and the nature of God respectively; together they outline the new boundaries of the phenomenon of man.

The God of the Old Testament—detached, full of wrath, and beyond our reach—and the physics of Newton—objective, cold, and separating the cosmos from the individual human being—share the same matrix, which is the *matrix of separation*. They also make the human being small, lost, insignificant. We are pitiful against the inscrutable God-Father, Jehovah. We are equally pitiful against the inexorable laws of nature of Mr. Newton.

In short, the old physics and the old theology spelled out confinement. At the root of this confinement was the separation of God from man, and the separation of the physical universe from the human universe: the outer and the inner were galaxies apart.

The assumption behind my arguments is that we may have been too much influenced—if only subconsciously—by the Old Testament, in *creating* physics and other forms of knowledge about the universe. Newtonian physics was a product of the pre-evolution era. Hence its findings are expressed in absolute terms. The conceptual blinders imposed on us by the bequeathed theology were just too great to allow Newton, or anyone else for that matter, to contemplate the world along the lines of the 20th century New Physics. There is a theological undercurrent which runs parallel to the visible story of classical physics.

Only after we have loosened our minds to permit ourselves to see the world not as a rigid framed picture—framed according to God's preestablished design—only then could we consider the story of the world to be a running film; and only then could we contemplate the species as evolving. Before that time, the conceptual and theological blocks did not allow us to *imagine* differently, to *conceive* differently, to *perceive* differently. Imagination, conception, and perception are all connected. Darwin began to perceive. The theological blocks at his time were already loosened. It is important to emphasize however that Darwin was not Mr. Evolution. He rendered compellingly but only one aspect of evolution—the evolution of the species through adaptation (biological evolution).

We are now beginning to see a larger picture emerging, the picture of the Western mind getting out of the predetermined frame and venturing to see the vistas of the world evolving. Let's recapitulate the story. We first assumed that the earth was created as we see it at present. We simultaneously assumed that all species were created as they appear to us now. We furthermore assumed that all physics is given to us as a package, once and for all. We simultaneously assumed that God was a fixed frame, the frame that holds everything firm and immutable.

Now we are discovering that physics, and by implication all science, is not given to us but continually *created by us*—something that exemplifies the creative and evolving powers of the human mind. We are also slowly beginning to perceive that our God is evolving as well.

The New Physics and the New Theology spell out liberation. The name of this liberation is creativeness within the compass of evolution unfolding, and within the compass of our unfolding understanding.

Let's clearly see that the New Physics is not a local affair of physicists or even confined to the vicissitudes of science. Especially it is not the story of the old paradigm breaking down, and the new paradigm having a hard time of establishing itself. It is something far more significant. It is a story involving the third stage of evolution, of recognizing that science, and all our cognitive products, must be viewed as a part of the evolving film as well; it is a story of the recognition that we are both viewers and the makers of the film.

Furthermore the New Theology, which I call Eco-theology—a creation-oriented theology, as distinguished from old Christian theologies which are redemption-oriented—is again not a matter to be confined to the theological hair-splitting of the churches; neither is it a matter of breaking down the old theological paradigm—that is, after Nietzsche announced that God is dead[1]—but is a matter of recognizing that all is evolving, including God. Originally God was the fixed frame, the frame that holds everything firm. Now with evolution conceived as a running film, we no longer have any fixed frames. The time has arrived to look at the evolving nature of the Framer. This is what I call the fourth stage of evolution, one that encompasses the theological or the transcendental dimension as well.

Finally, the New Physics and the New Theology are not two separate developments, to be understood in their own specific terms, but parts of the same larger process of unfreezing, or the process of becoming, so that we can say that human knowledge and human spirituality—including religion and images of God—are subject to the same all-pervading evolutionary flow. We have to have the courage of accepting the ultimate consequences of the evolutionary perspective.

The Newtonian paradigm, as the ultimate frame, was already profoundly in doubt at the end of the 19th century when such phenomena as radiation were clearly outside the frame. With Einstein, we tried to mend the old frame and maintain that the bigger relativistic frame was correct, and that it contained in itself the Newtonian picture. But the new enlarged frame was problem-ridden from the start: it suggested many counter-intuitive notions; besides, as a frame, it had

---

[1] See *Gay Science* (1882), sections 108 ("God is dead"), 125 ("Whither is God? ... We have killed him, you and I"), and 343 ("The greatest recent event—that 'God is dead,' that the belief in the Christian god has become unbelievable—is already beginning to cast its first shadows over Europe.")

fuzzy edges. We have never been comfortable with it. Our common sense has been shaped by the Newtonian language and conceptions. Still, with Einstein, we have a frame—a bit open-ended and not quite precisely delineating its territory, but something to hold to.

With the New Physics, we are in a new situation. We don't have the frame given to us, which we can happily accept, elaborate, and say: all is well, we have got a set of laws and theories which hold objectively and universally; they depict the permanent order out there. We know that the ultimate elementary particles are not so ultimate; and that they may not be particles either—in the physical sense of the word. At least on the level of quantum physics, we process reality around us according to the nature of our cognitive faculties; according to the nature of our theories; according to the nature of our instruments. The process and the processor become one. The observer and the observed merge. We have also recognized that objectivity is a form of myth. The idea of 'objective' facts, and of particles which we—as it were—photograph in our theories and in our descriptions, is now seen as a glorified fiction.

As mind is evolving and recreating itself, it produces new frames, which are but externalized images of mind processing reality—now in this way, now in another way. All products of our understanding are necessarily shaped according to the nature of our mind, its propensities and capacities at a given time. Our mind is present in each and every theory and frame. We always look *at our mind* when we look at the world. What we see, when we look through the Newtonian frame, is our own mind built into this frame. *The process of frame-making is the process of mind-making.* At one point it makes sense to say that the world and the mind are co-extensive, as I have tried to argue in my essay "A Model of Reality as Mind".[2] If mind is a part of the evolutionary process, then there is every reason to believe that future science, future forms of understanding, may be vastly different from what they are now. We constantly and inevitably co-create the world. This is the scintillatingly liberating message of the New Physics.

At this point we may return to the New Theology. When our world is constantly co-created, our God cannot be frozen and static. If we accept the consequences of the New Physics—that we live in a participatory universe—then the whole idea of a fixed God and redemption theology look like a shadow of the past epoch. Only when the world is given to us, and it is brutish and nasty, and we are helpless in it, only then we must be saved from it, we must be redeemed. Since we have no powers to redeem ourselves, we have to be redeemed by God. The old God is given, static, inscrutable. We are frail and our nature is weak. The Messiah is particularly welcome in this context. Whether he will come or not, it is comforting to think that he might. But there is no Messiah in Eco-theology, as I will argue in the course of this essay.

The program of 17th century secularism was undoubtedly bold and far reaching, and so were new

---

2 In *Old and New Questions in Physics, Cosmology, Philosophy, and Theoretical Biology* (A. van der Merwe, ed.), 1983.

dreams of Reason of the 18th century. However, all these new designs of Secularism were only perpetuating the theology of Redemption. All the secular dreams of the post-Renaissance Western society, including Marxism, and including the American Dream, are variations on the theme of redemption theology: they are mythical vessels created for our individual salvation.

It is quite different within the New Theology or, to use my terms, Eco-theology. The world is in the process of perpetual becoming. Therefore, imperfect as we are, we redeem ourselves through our own creative effort, by creating meaning within ourselves, by co-creating the universe, by creating ourselves in the image of God... who is in the making in us. We are God-in-the-making, in the sense that the universe is in the making, partly by being received and processed in our minds. We create realities, both social and physical, including the reality of our mind—through which we create further the world around us—either in the image of Grace or in the image of the machine. If the former is the case, we live in God's universe; if the latter, we are in the world dictated by the machine.

The creative act becomes all-important for joining together the New Physics, Eco-theology, and our individual quest for meaning. We redeem the human condition, the fact of living in the participatory universe and the idea of God evolving in us, by enacting the creative act. At the beginning was creation. And all life is creation. The end will come when creation will cease. Creativity is a gift. But it is also a curse; we are doomed to it—if we are to maintain our status as God's messengers.

The idea of God-in-the-making in us may sound strange or even offensive to those who are used to thinking of Him as a benevolent unchanging entity, benignly overlooking our vicissitudes. But to see Him overlooking us is to go back to a fixed frame, is to relinquish our responsibility for ourselves, is to relegate our powers of creation onto Him. When all frames are dissolved, and instead we have a continuously running film, we have changed a constant God for an evolving one. This is a consequence of a radically evolutionary approach. So often we have accepted evolution but only in its fragmentary manifestations. Yet nothing is excluded from its flow: it must be seen through the working of the geo-sphere, through the working of the bio-sphere, through the working of the nous-sphere, through the metamorphosis of the theo-sphere.

In short, to recognize evolution without evasion is to recognize the evolution of our comprehension, or of our understanding; it is to recognize the transient character of all our tools, including the tools with which we think, those very concepts and processes through which we grasp, and thus understand the physical world around us; including also those ideas and concepts with which we think of God and through which we understand God. As our understanding evolves, so it renders different shapes of reality, including the reality of God.

Throughout this chapter, I have attempted to show that in re-making ourselves, in bringing about the New

Paradigm, we have to re-make the entire conceptual fabric within which we think, imagine, and evaluate things. In the process, we have to change our notion of knowledge and our concept of God—all of this as a part of evolution unfolding.

CHAPTER 4

MESSIAH, SELF-PERFECTIBILITY, AND ECO-THEOLOGY

WHEN WE look at Eastern religions (Hinduism, Buddhism, and Taoism) vis-a-vis Christianity, we are immediately struck that these religions are not overshadowed by the concept of the Messiah. This fact is of immense importance, but usually overlooked. In the Judeo-Christian traditions, the Messiah is always in the background. He will come to save us all. He will redeem. We wait for him. We always wait for another to save us. We always think that salvation, spiritual or political, is a public act to be performed by a chosen one. We want to be saved by someone—not by ourselves.

This attitude toward salvation has enormous consequences. Traditional religion may have waned; the idea of the Messiah has not. For even at the time when the idea of church-the-redeemer (or more specifically: Jesus-the-redeemer) has lost its liturgic power, we have not stopped thinking in messianic terms, in terms of one saving the many. In truth, we have elevated *science* and *technology* to the role of the savior. The tenacity with which we cling to the old idea of the savior is truly amazing. The Messiah, of one sort or another, will come from the outside and save us—no matter what. This idea permeates the whole culture, although at times it is expressed in strange terms.

If you consider the idea of the 'technological fix,' then you become aware that it is indeed a residue of messianic thinking. And finally take the Bomb. It is a form of radical salvation—though it may be of a perverted kind. The Bomb will clean it all; and will end all our troubles. In our murky subconscious, we sometimes think of the Bomb as the 'final solution.' This is a residue of messianic thinking... grown into a pathology.

Insofar as the messianic theology has developed into the expectation to wait for someone to redeem us, it has indirectly cultivated irresponsibility in our midst. The whole phenomenon of modern technology, which will fix it all, is a disaster both existentially and theologically: the scope of our responsibilities has been continually shrinking as we have been waiting for the fixes. It has been a disaster theologically, too, for we have delegated our salvation to a rather savage and insensitive God, which I call *Technos*. It cannot be denied that the very ideal of the Messiah is built into the structure of our present technology. The idea that a form of irresponsibility is built into the notion of the Messiah is not going to be palatable to Christian theologians. Yet we must face the issue squarely. In the concept of the savior, there is at least a lingering notion that we ourselves cannot take responsibility for our own salvation.

It is all different in Eastern religions: no Messiah to come, no one to save you. You yourself must be your own Messiah: through good Karma, through following the path of virtuous life, through achieving Enlightenment which will mean the end of suffering. When the Buddha lay dying, he said:

> It may be that, in some of you, the thought will arise: The word of the master is ended; we have no teacher more. But it is not thus that you should regard it. The dharma (teaching) which I have given you, let that be your teacher when I am gone.

Even the Buddhas do but point the way.

Yes, even the Buddhas do but point the way. Let us realize that, at later times, Buddhism did become the doctrine of faith at the expense of the older doctrine of merit. The devotional life, simple faith and prayer, were deemed all-important for salvation, not the hard spiritual path of self-perfectibility. But this devotional path is characteristic only for some forms of Buddhism, while its main thrust emphasizes the path of merit, of personal responsibility, of being your own savior. Vis-a-vis this main thrust of Buddhism, we cannot but notice the irresponsible side of Christianity: of always waiting for the Big One to come and salvage you.

Waiting for the other to save you is a denial of your authenticity and your responsibility. Working on yourself is an expression of the trust in your self-perfectibility. Those who have worked on their spiritual path not only can help themselves; they also emanate with this subtle radiance which we call *grace,* and which helps others. There is no question that the path of spiritual self-development has been known within the Christian tradition. Yet it has not been sufficiently realized that the idea of the savior that will save us all contains more than a germ of our own disempowerment, of apathy, and indirectly, of irresponsibility.

Let me now go directly to some of the basic tenets of Eco-theology. It should be abundantly clear that Individual Responsibility is of paramount importance. You must assume responsibility for all, including future generations. In the connected world, guided by the ecological perception of wholeness and the sense of interrelatedness, any responsible ethic must include the responsibility for future generations.

However, the sense of responsibility is a rather subtle notion. There is no logical necessity, or even natural necessity, to assume responsibility. Responsibility is individually decided upon and individually carried through; or not carried through. It is not an economic category. Indeed, economic thinking rather suppresses than encourages it. It is not a philosophical category. Philosophy can analyze its meaning but is usually powerless to help us to acquire it. In order to possess this larger sense of responsibility, you must have a larger sense of the cosmos, and you must find your own place within it.

To be human is to live in the state of responsibility. Furthermore, you must be on a continuous journey of self-transcendence or Self-Perfectibility.

CHAPTER 5

An important part of our overall responsibility is the responsibility for our inner life. It is the responsibility for our ceaseless journey of becoming, a continuous journey of self-transcendence, or self-perfectibility. Seen in this light, responsibility is an aspect of our spirituality. This statement can be challenged. Secular humanists and atheists may claim that they not only know the meaning of responsibility; they can claim that they exercise it while rejecting spirituality.

The important point to notice is that spirituality is not necessarily a function of religion and does not have to be tied to any religion. To conceive of intrinsic human meaning as *sui generis*, as irreducible to things economic or physical—furthermore, to take care of this meaning, not only in your own life but in the life of others—is to exercise responsibility within a spiritual framework. Therefore, you can be a secular humanist, or even an atheist, and act within a framework of spirituality—although usually it is a difficult act; at times a collapsing act; as the intrinsic human meaning needs justification which goes beyond the concept of man as the measure of all things. The saying that, "for man, the root of man is man himself" (Marx[1]) does not give us very deep roots. Our roots stretch beyond man—to embrace the cosmos.

Spirituality is not an expression of romantic nostalgia for the things of the past, for religion of the past; nor is it a spurious superficial trapping, empty ritual connected with things unseen and unimportant. Spirituality is a vessel within which most important

---

[1] Introduction to *Critique of Hegel's Philosophy of Right* (1843).

characteristics of human beings as human are contained, and through which they are perpetuated. Spirituality is a safeguard of not only the sanctity of life that we consider sacred, but also of life itself.

Unless you have reverence for life, you cannot have dignity and grace. And unless you have dignity and grace, you cannot have meaning in life. Graceless life, life deprived of dignity, is not the one that can be meaningful. Spirituality provides the means and the framework within which transcendental aspirations of man, grace, dignity, reverence for life, all reside. Those characteristics are the ones which are indispensable for life endowed with meaning. Consequently, spirituality conceived as a vessel containing the most precious attributes of human existence is a necessary condition of a meaningful life. In short, life endowed with meaning is one that always embraces some dimensions of spirituality. If such is the case, then spirituality is a rational expression of the human condition. Spirituality is a state of mind; really, a state of being. In this state, we experience the world as if it were endowed with grace, because we are then ourselves endowed with grace.

Let me now introduce the third element, which I call Brahman Consciousness or Brahman Enlightenment, the ultimate stage of the projected journey of our Self Perfectibility. As man thinks, so he becomes, say the Upanishads. "Adore, and what you adore, try to become" (Aurobindo). "In truth, who knows God becomes God" (Mundaka Upanishad). Those are the statements projecting our being into what we are not yet. They should not be treated literally, but rather as guide-posts helping our inner journey. In order to be, we have to enlarge our being continually. In order to enlarge our being, we must have a place to go—not in a trivial economic sense, but in a cosmic sense. In order to penetrate the non-trivial aspects of our being, the sacred aspects of our being, we must have a sacred realm with which we are connected. Our eschaton, the sense of ultimate purpose, cannot be grounded in our economic worries.

Let's summarize our discussion so far. We can retain the idea of the Messiah but in a new sense of the term. Eco-theology maintains that if we wish to retain the image of the Messiah, then Messiah is equal to evolution unfolding and redeeming itself and redeeming everything else as it reaches the state of consummation (Omega Point of Teilhard). Evolution is God-in-the-making. At this juncture of cosmic history, before higher evolutionary forms emerge and supersede us as more efficient vehicles of God making, we are God-in-the-making. Hence it is of great importance that we maintain our individual responsibility, that we keep on the journey of self-perfectibility and that we aspire to Brahman Enlightenment.

In minimal terms, outlined here is a *methodological program*: how to make more of a universe that is nurturing God, how to make more of ourselves while continually fusing meaning into our lives. Messiah equals Evolution, which is the function of our Individual Responsibility, which in turn implies Self-Perfectibility, which in turn implies the quest for Brahman Consciousness.

CHAPTER 5

RESPONSIBILITY REVISITED

ALL MODELS are inadequate. They are convenient boxes into which we try to press the variety of life, and of our understanding of it, so that we can see more clearly the patterns and arrangements. All systems of theology are models; in this sense they are inadequate. Instead of building a whole system, I have proposed a methodology. Its purpose is not to solve all our problems, and in particular present theological knots and controversies; its purpose is rather, as the Buddha said, "to point the way."

Individual Responsibility is a most important element, and it needs further comments. It is clear that a sense of responsibility is not enough in itself. It must go hand in hand with a right eschaton, a larger purpose on behalf of which this responsibility is exercised. At some point, responsibility has to become a religious concept.

When the sense of responsibility is wedded to and inspired by a wrong eschaton, or by a perverted sense of ultimate purpose, then tragedies may follow, as happened in Hitler's Germany, Stalin's Russia, or El

Salvador in the early 1980s. What therefore is needed is universal consciousness or Brahman Consciousness, a sense of unity with all, a feeling of empathy for all, in short, a framework of universal altruism. When the framework is informed by compassion and inspired by a sense of co-working with evolution, to elicit its further spiritual dimensions, then the sense of individual responsibility will not breed madmen.

As I said before, responsibility which goes beyond one's selfish concerns cannot be justified rationally. There is no reason why one should feel responsible and act responsibly on behalf of all humanity and of evolution. Responsibility is ultimately a concept that belongs to the sacred, as it informs us who we ultimately are, and what is our purpose.

The same holds for the idea of Self-Perfectibility and Brahman-Enlightenment. They belong to the sacred too. In a subtle way, they support each other and articulate each other. Responsibility without a larger cosmos would make no sense. The larger cosmos without human meaning, and without the process of self-actualization, would make no sense either. The very idea of 'making sense' is a part of our spiritual striving.

The phenomenon of humanity is as natural in this cosmos as it is supernatural. The sacred and the natural merge together, are parts—perhaps even aspects—of the same structure. Evolution is making molecules, is making minds, is making sacred symbols. The natural and the sacred are one because the sacred is an outcome of the natural process—of evolution making sacred symbols and making gods. In this sense, evolution is God.

To say that the natural and the sacred are one is not to blur all distinctions or to deny the obvious: that a tree branch is one thing, and a Gregorian chant is another. The aesthetic and spiritual aspects of human activity, mystic poetry, and great sacred texts are natural manifestations of the mind and yet so 'miraculous' that they seem to belong to another realm. However, it is the same mind that perceives the ordinary and conceives of the extraordinary; that perceives a tree and is awed by the Chartres Cathedral.

There is a continuous dialogue between the immanent and the transcendent in us. Traditional religions placed the transcendent in the original heaven from which we have fallen. To transcend the trivia of our daily existence meant to return to our original grace. Yet this is the transcendence going backward.

Eco-theology reverses the process and conceives of transcendence as going forward, to that which we have not yet been—for such is the true meaning of transcendence. All Evolution is transcendence going forward, whereby particular immanent daily actions are redeemed on a higher level of evolutionary attainment. The symbol of highest transcendence—God—must be conceived in the same manner, as transcendence going forward. God as a truly transcendent reality suggests a state which is so far beyond us that we shall have to go far, far beyond ourselves to reach him.

CHAPTER 6

PAUL TILLICH AND THE
ECOLOGY OF HOPE

OUR EXAMINATION of Eco-theology would be incomplete without mentioning the importance of the theologian Paul Tillich (1886-1965) and his idea of courage; and without visiting, if ever so briefly, the ecology of hope.

Man, for Tillich, is not what he is and *as he is*, but what he *essentially* is. Essence is understood by Tillich as that what man potentially is. The real transition should be one from existence to essence. What happens in our daily life is the reverse transition: from essence to existence. During the process we become estranged from ourselves; from our better selves that is, from our potential selves.

This is not much different from Plato, who claimed that while human essence is embodied in a particular existence, the soul is entrapped and coarsened, and thus loses its vision, its clarity, its potential. Tillich protests that his is not a repetition of the Platonic idea. If so, then essence-existence relationship must be construed in evolutionary terms: we have not yet fully actualized our potency, the possibility latent in us—to that extent, our existence is 'sordid,' never entirely up to what we may become—in the evolutionary journey that is. The whole predicament was beautifully summarized two centuries earlier by Goethe:

> To treat man as he is
> Is to debase him
> To treat man as he ought to be
> Is to engrace him[1]

The way man actualizes his essential self is through the peculiarity of the structure of his being. Hence ontology was of utmost importance to Tillich's thought. Ontology was for Tillich the basic ground from which to start one's inquiry into the human nature and into the nature of religion. He wrote:

> Man occupies a preeminent position in ontology, not as an outstanding object among other objects, but as that being who asks the ontological question and, in whose self-awareness, the ontological answer can be found.[2]

---

[1] This is a paraphrase. The exact quote by Goethe, from his work *Wilhelm Meisters Lehrjahre* (1795), is this: *Wenn wir sagtest Du, die Menschen nur nehmen, wie sie sind, so machen wir sie schlechter; wenn wir sie behandeln als wären sie, was sie sein sollten, so bringen wir sie dahin, wohin sie zu bringen sind.* In translation: "When we take people merely as they are, we make them worse; when we treat them as if they were what they should be, we improve them as far as they can be improved."

[2] *Systematic Theology*, vol. 1 (1951: 168). 'Ontology' refers to the study of fundamental reality.

CHAPTER 6

The ethical question concerning the nature of courage, and the ontological question concerning the nature of being, are intimately and inextricably woven together:

> [A]n understanding of courage presupposes an understanding of man and of his world, its structures and values. Only he who knows this knows what to affirm and what to negate. The ethical question of the nature of courage leads inescapably to the ontological question of the nature of being. And the procedure can be reversed. The ontological question of the nature of being can be asked as the ethical question of the nature of courage. Courage can show us what being is, and being can show us what courage is.[3]

The question of courage is by no means theoretical or theological. Western scholars live nowadays in comfort and freedom, with their jobs well secured, and with their pensions well provided for. Yet courage is totally lacking in Western universities. 'Intellectual' courage is not courage but hiding behind the screen of established orthodoxies. The roots of real courage are invariably moral. Present academics, by and large, have no firm moral convictions. Living by the creed of rationality leads to an atrophy of courage in a deeper sense of the term. As they do not have it themselves, they cannot instill courage in their students. Thus we are breeding, on the campuses, a spineless generation, with no

---

[3] *The Courage to Be* (1952: 2).

courage and no moral sense; the two are connected; and the consequences are devastating.[4]

The 'courage to be' is for Tillich one of the most fundamental attributes of human existence. Yet this courage needs an evolutionary dimension. A unique feature of our humanness in us is not only the 'courage to be' but the 'courage to *become*,' to continually transcend every station we have reached. The 'courage to become' is one of the defining characteristics of Eco-theology.

An understanding of this courage to transcend gives us a unique perspective on the nature of man and his values, and of this world and its structure. Only he who knows that to be a human being means not only the courage to be but also the courage to build beyond, the courage to leave behind every station we have arrived at, will understand the agony and beauty of past strivings, either of individuals or societies or species; as well he will understand present frustrations and despairs that we are not able to do more than we can actually do. We rationally understand our limitations, but in our deeper instinct, in our transcendent vision, we know that we can and must overcome these limitations, as our destiny is nothing short of divine.

The right understanding of the courage to be and the courage to become leads us to the *ecology of hope*. Hope is the foundation of our courage—the 'hope eternal,' in

---

[4] This striking indictment of modern academia is echoed in Skolimowski's other writings. See, for example, *Theatre of the Mind* (1984: 130-132) and his essay "Rationality, knowledge, and violence" (in *Knowledge, Reality, and Happiness*, Mishra and Sagar, eds., 1991).

spite of all the vicissitudes of our fortune. The restoration of hope is particularly important in our times, eaten by skepticism and nihilism. In restoring hope, we demonstrate responsibility in action. The ecology of hope must be tenderly cultivated amidst the ecology of destruction. Indeed, it looks as though a destructive demon has created its own ecology, which is a downward spiral sucking us into the center of the abyss.

Hope is a prelude to grace. Withering of hope is a prelude to death. How can a people live who do not live in hope? Hope is the spring that renews us daily. Hope is as fundamental as the oxygen we breathe. Hope is the scaffolding of our very being. Hope is the ray of light that separates life from death. We must burn the candle of hope like an act of self-sacrifice.

Like Lazarus, we must rise from our broken condition to embrace the new dawn of hope, which is the light of our human condition, and without which our human condition is steeped in darkness.

Hope and faith are ontological underpinnings of our being. Our rational mind seems to have forgotten that faith and hope are not foolish indulgencies of 'weak' people who are not tough enough to confront the world in a tough way, but the very roots that nurture our being.

In Peter Shaffer's play *Equus* we are confronted with a line: "Without worship, man shrinks." The ecology of hope goes a step further, as it maintains that if you worship nothing, you are nothing. 'To believe' is natural for human beings; as well as to worship something.

Faith, hope, and reverence are therefore the necessary ingredients of our well-being; they are integral dimensions of our wholeness.

We now clearly see that wholeness and hope are connected. In hope we bring wholeness to our being. Hope and wholeness are metaphysical foundations of our life. To understand these foundations is to enter the realm of theology. And conversely, to understand the nature of religion is to understand the structure of our hope and wholeness, and the role they play in our existence.

In brief, hope is a mode of our being. A healthy human being cannot live outside the gentle mantle of hope. Hope is a pre-condition of our mental health. It is also the awareness that human destiny is not determined by blind destructive forces that will crush us no matter what. Hope is a reassertion of our belief in the meaning of human life, and in the sense of the universe. Most importantly, hope is a pre-condition of all meaning, of all strivings, of feeling at home in this confused and complex world of ours. Thus, endorsing hope is not a form of foolishness but a form of wisdom.

CHAPTER 7

GRACE

WHAT IS the place of Grace within Eco-theology? Grace does not come to those who do not invite it, who are not ready for it, who do not work for it. Yet oftentimes it does not come to those who work for it and invite it. In this sense, grace is a gift. But is it a supernatural gift or a part of our natural endowment? Christian theology will insist that it is the former; Eco-theology maintains that it is the latter.

Is a gift of grace more special than a gift of music? At first we are inclined to say 'yes'. Upon deeper reflection, the answer is not so obvious. Was Mozart not in a state of grace when he composed his most celestial pieces? And why do we call them 'celestial'? Clearly because, at some point, a great musical talent is a form of grace. Yet we are not inclined to call a musical talent a supernatural gift. When Michelangelo was sculpting his greatest pieces, we would be equally inclined to say that he was in a state of grace. Yet an artistic talent is not considered a supernatural gift; rather, a part of the natural human endowment. We are all gifted musically—to a degree. Some are gifted to an extraordinary degree.

Might it not be reasonable to suggest that we are all endowed with, at least, some rudiments of grace? Some are endowed more, some are endowed less. And some indeed work extraordinarily hard to bring the latent grace in them to full blossom. Grace, like a great musical talent, has to be nurtured, trained, and developed in order to come to fruition. The story of grace as revelation omits to tell us the endless toils, the great discipline, the endless exercises that the illustrious ones had gone through before they achieved the state of grace. The Buddha wandered for three years, fasting nearly to death, before he was visited by Enlightenment and then lived in the state of grace. Jesus 'disappeared' for 18 years—possibly spending most of this time in an Essene community. Doing what? We don't know. Probably not carpentry, but some strenuous spiritual exercises.

In short, great spiritual leaders were supreme because of an extraordinary exertion of their will power in eliciting their potential for grace. We, ordinary human beings, so often fail not because we do not have this potential in us but because we do not have the will power, the fantastic discipline, the inner resilience to keep going—no matter what obstacles ordinary reality puts in our path.

In this sense, grace is the result of good karma, or right karma, the fruit of one's inner workings—a part of the natural endowment brought to an extraordinary fruition. There is no royal road to grace, or a set of prescribed exercises. Our spiritual life is too subtle and too complex to produce grace as the result of some specific exercises. However, we know that the chosen ones invariably went through rigorous spiritual practices. So the inner discipline and spiritual practices are a necessary condition, but not a sufficient one.

Within the Christian tradition, grace is viewed as given from above, a gift of God. This conception may be seen as a form of salvation: a little Messiah (called Grace) is planted within ourselves, almost irrespective of our merit. Grace in this context is a form of salvation or redemption—by the forces outside ourselves.

The position of Eco-theology is quite different. We must be our own source of grace. Grace is to be conceived as a part of our overall responsibility. We don't want to be deprived of this part of our responsibility which leads to Grace. This is not a reassertion of human arrogance but a consistent stand which maintains that we are 'doomed' to our responsibility. This responsibility, as we have argued, is ultimately religious in nature.

When I look at our religion, and especially Christianity, from the perspective of the year 3000 AD, I see it as profoundly changed. We shall become favorite children of God by assuming more and more responsibility; and by exercising it. In this sense Eco-theology is an expression of God's evolutionary design. And who is going to question God's inscrutable design, if God indeed is inscrutable? What the prophets have done in the past was to judge, on the basis of a bit of the design, the whole design. We cannot do more. But we should not try to do less. The shape of religion in the year 3000 will be fantastically different from what it is now. It's with this in mind that we have to start designing new images of God now.

Finally we should ask: What *is* grace? What does it mean to be in a state of grace? Such questions are never easy to answer. While pondering over this question, I was sitting in a garden and listening to Cesar Franck's piano sonata. A dog came close to me, visibly wanting to be stroked. I asked myself "Can a dog be in a state of grace, and if not, why not?" Somehow the question appeared incongruous. But I have no evidence that a dog cannot be in a state of grace; especially if grace is a gift of heaven. Yet within the framework of Eco-theology, a dog cannot be in a state of grace. For grace is one of the uniquely human sensitivities. On the level of Homo sapiens, evolution has created self-consciousness, then spirituality, then this state of being we call grace.[1]

Grace is a condition of our being, a condition of our wholeness. But more than that, it is a condition of harmony with the cosmic plan; at least with the forces which transcend one's individual self. This condition of wholeness, which we call grace, invariably goes beyond the wholeness of one's individual being, beyond the integration within the human person. For grace radiates harmony which is of a cosmic kind. For this reason, we imagine its source to be in heaven, or simply a special gift of god. One of the characteristics of grace is that it is a form of love. Grace is also a form of radiance, which,

---

[1] For further discussion of the concept of mankind as defined by his sensitivities, see my book *Theatre of the Mind* (1984), especially Chapter One.

like hope, enables others, within its reach, to be more dignified, more human, closer to their inner selves.

The relationship between grace and responsibility is one of the most important problems of Christian theology, and perhaps of any theology. It can be argued that individual responsibility is a kind of gift. If so, responsibility can be conceived as a form of grace—if grace itself is a gift from outside. But this way of explaining is not very fruitful. For so often responsibility is felt as a burden, as carrying a cross for the sake of other things. It is more fruitful therefore to consider responsibility as a *vehicle*, as a means through which other things are accomplished, including grace. Grace is never a means, always an end. We are all endowed with responsibility. Without it, we are not fully human. Grace is something else. To acquire it is to be on the path of divinity.

Grace is the flower. In its radiance are reflected all other attainments of the human heart and spirit.

CHAPTER 8

TEILHARD'S PREDICAMENT

THE HISTORY of the Western Christian church has been nothing short of turbulent. The last century has seen the church at its low ebb. A time of crisis is also a time of reformers who attempt to put things aright. Of the many important Christian theologians of the 20th century, the following three should be mentioned: Schweitzer, Teilhard, and Tillich. Schweitzer (at least at his best) can be easily accommodated within Eco-theology. The heritage of Tillich has been discussed. In this chapter we shall discuss the ambiguous theological heritage of Teilhard de Chardin (1881-1955).

There are two opposite forces within Teilhard's theology which are never satisfactorily reconciled in his own writings. Teilhard's predicament is also Schweitzer's predicament; it is really the predicament of 20th century Christianity: how to reconcile the Christian teaching based on dogma, revelation, the idea of salvation, as well as the idea of the return to the Paradise, with the new insights, a new Tao that accentuates the process of self-perfectibility, of responsibility, of the idea of man/woman who co-create with God. In more explicit terms, we witness a clash between the past dogma and the realization of the Cosmic Christ in each of us; the clash between the authority imposed on us, and the sense of our own responsibility for our own life as well as for the life of the globe.

If we take Teilhard's chief opus *The Phenomenon of Man*, it is clear that his God is evolving toward the Omega Point; and only then, at Omega, will he become Full God. Such is the main thrust of the book. However, at the very end of the book, in the epilogue, Teilhard changes the whole perspective and, as it were, tries to 'mend' his ways and explicitly acknowledges that his Omega God is in the image of the traditional Christian God. This epilogue is a strange thing. After he has developed a new theological perspective, Teilhard 'catches' himself in heresy, becomes aware of his schism, and proposes to return to Christianity. It thus appears that Teilhard forced himself to reinterpret his creative evolution in the Christian key, as he writes:

The universe fulfilling itself in a synthesis of centres in perfect conformity with the laws of union. God, the Centre of centres. In that final vision, the Christian dogma culminates. And so exactly, so perfectly does this coincide with the Omega Point that doubtless I should never have ventured to envisage the latter or formulate the hypothesis rationally if, in my consciousness as a believer, I had not found not only its speculative model but also its living reality. (p. 294)

Teilhard tries to equate the process of evolutionary unfolding with the Christo-Genesis. But the equation does not work because it cannot work. The two processes of conceiving of God—the traditional Christian and the evolutionary—are diametrically opposed to each other. The respective eschatologies are different too. We shall not belabor the differences in the story of creation. Far more important is the source of the divine, the idea of salvation, the ultimate concept of man. By attempting to subsume Omega Point under Christian theology, Teilhard undermines the *raison d'être* of evolution as an unfolding and self-actualizing process. For if evolution is a return to Christ, a return to the original Paradise, then it only recapitulates the past. If, on the other hand, evolution is actualizing itself, and will be only actualized at the end of time, then there is no return to the Paradise Lost, for there never was a Paradise before.

Let me discuss this dilemma in some detail, for it is of great importance. If we recognize the notion and the authority of God as conceived in the traditional religions, particularly in traditional Christianity, then our evolution, including the moral and spiritual one, is completed. What we can do, and the only thing we can do, is to return to the Paradise Lost, to reacquire virtues that have been bestowed on us by God-the-Original-Maker.

If, on the other hand, we see ourselves as unfinished spiritual beings, indeed only in the infancy of our evolution, then we simply cannot accept the notion of the traditional God who made us perfect. When we contemplate our primordial beginnings in the cosmic dust, we realize that they were far from godly. It is only at the end of the Immense Journey that we may become godly; but only if we actualize God in ourselves. God is in the making—in us. The further we go in our evolutionary journey, the closer we may approach Him. *God is spiritually actualizing itself in us.* Our goal should therefore be to transcend further and further and never to return. For a return represents fall from grace. Evolution is a barbed wire. If we could return, it would be a return to brutishness and dimness and not to grace and perfection. Insofar as Teilhard upholds the Christian myth of Return, he profoundly undermines his evolutionary thesis. Insofar as he seriously upholds the evolutionary thesis, he profoundly undermines Christian heritage. There is thus a profound incoherence in his views.

But there is a way of incorporating the Christo-Genesis into the evolutionary design, namely by treating Jesus not as God, a point of final destiny and of ultimate strivings, but as a symbol, as an inspiration, as a reminder that even at this stage of our evolutionary development we are capable of so much grace and divinity. Then Christ-consciousness becomes not so much the ritualistic identification with Christ's body or blood but an imaginary flame that illumines our roads towards greater grace and consciousness; it becomes a constant reminder of that which we are capable.

Another path to reconciliation is to think of the whole universe in a sacramental way—the view not entirely foreign to early Christianity but not one that is actively entertained and pursued by present churches.

Our culture is woven around the skeleton of Christianity. To deny or destroy this skeleton would be nothing short of destroying Western culture.[1] Cultures live by symbols. Symbols of our culture have been thoroughly pervaded by Christian teaching and metaphors. We cannot tear apart the vessel in which we are floating. Like Descartes, we have to reconstruct our boat while we are afloat.

Our task is made even more difficult by such people as Lynn White, who has insisted that the blueprint for the destruction of the environment is the Bible. In his celebrated 1967 essay, "The Historical Roots of our Ecologic Crisis",[2] White has galvanized our attention, and almost paralyzed us with inaction, by telling us that, in a sense, we are doomed. The most important document of our culture, by which we have lived, is fundamentally misconceived. As a guidance and inspiration, it had led us astray. White has eloquently argued that the Judeo-Christian theology is responsible for the separation of man from nature. "Man's relation to the soil was profoundly changed. Formerly man had been part of nature; now he was the exploiter of nature. ... Man and nature are two things, and man is master."

Here therefore was the evidence showing that the sacred book was, if only implicitly, a blueprint for destruction. During the last 15 years, we have absorbed the shock of this 'revelation' and slowly have learned to live with it. We have come to recognize that our culture

---

[1] Indeed, some have recently attempted just such a deconstruction of Christianity. See, for example, David Skrbina's *The Jesus Hoax* (2019).

[2] *Science* 155(3767): 1203-1207.

is not made of one cloth but possesses various layers and is open to different interpretations. What we have witnessed during the last decade is a conscious effort, both within the Judaic and Christian traditions, to reinterpret our religious and cultural heritage, so that we can make peace with nature, and thus with an important part of ourselves.

CHAPTER 9

THE CHURCHES' AWAKENING

ACCORDING to Tom Berry, a philosopher and a religious thinker, the churches have done close to zero in terms of rethinking their position vis a vis the ecological perspective. Yet the wind of change is slowly engulfing us all. Even within the churches, one hears the new whisperings which, though shy and timid, are potentially significant and powerful.

In the late 1970s. the American Baptist Ministry produced a brochure entitled ECO-JUSTICE, in which we read:

> Eco-justice means joining together concerns for ecology and justice. It expresses the age-old dream that "Earth shall be fair, and all her people wise" (as in Isaiah 11).
>
> Ecology deals with the interdependence of all forms of life. It reminds us that every living thing is a creature, a created being—women and men, animals, birds, fish, and plants. As each strand of a spider web is joined to another, all creatures are joined together in great webs of life. We draw our

sustenance from land and sea. We die. Our dust returns to the earth.

Justice focuses on human beings in relationship to each other. We are one with other creatures, but we are different, too. We are created in the Lord's image. Though God cares about all creatures, each person is of special worth in the sight of God.

Each person knows the meaning of justice. Each of us wants to be treated with respect. Each wants to 'have a say' in matters affecting one's self. Each wants to have a fair share of food, clothing, and other necessities.

This was a significant effort to rethink the whole net of relationships, including the problems of 'haves' and 'have-nots,' of extinction of species, of malnutrition, of inflation, of cancer as environmental disease—all along the ecological lines.

Out of this effort, or perhaps independently of it, came the declaration of the National Council of Churches in January 1980, which took a strong stand in favor of ecological justice, arguing that "perversion of *dominion* into *domination* (of nature) is a sin and one of the underlying causes of the energy crisis."

One might think that the Catholic Church, being most dominated by a hierarchical structure, would be most inhibited in taking new initiatives. A joint statement of Catholic bishops in the U.S.A.—against nuclear war—issued in 1982 (although weakened in its final wording) was a denial of this inhibition and a return to a Theology of the Earth. It was an assertion of the presence of God on this earth, particularly when the bishops argued that "Nuclear idolatry is profoundly anti-Christian." When the bishops were told, by the White House, to keep away from politics, they replied that the saving of the earth is no longer a political matter but a theological issue *par excellence*. This was indeed a salutary stand.

In some Catholic quarters, the new thinking goes even further.[1] The Eleventh Commandment Fellowship was established in San Francisco in 1981. Its purpose is to awaken "within each individual, of a deeply religious and spiritual response to the dangers of today's global ecological crisis," as well as to seek "the necessary steps to reverse the earth's present spiritual-ecological imbalance." Now, what is the Eleventh Commandment?

THE EARTH IS THE LORD'S AND THE FULLNESS THEREOF: THOU SHALL NOT DESPOIL THE EARTH, NOR DESTROY LIFE THEREON.

This is again a statement of Eco-theology. More interestingly still, the Eleventh Commandment, as formulated by its proponents, is not an abstract principle but is backed by appropriate guidelines for action:

1) Make the Eleventh Commandment the foundation of your personal ethic of the environment.

---

[1] Rossi, Vincent. "The Eleventh Commandment: Toward an ethic of ecology." *Epiphany* 1 (1981: 2-18).

2) Learn all you can about the ecological crisis so you will be able to make informed choices.

3) Become familiar with the many ecological appropriate techniques, practices, and devices that are being developed. Find ways to use them in your own life.

4) Examine your life. Begin to eliminate habits or activities that are destructive to the environment, no matter how slight. Begin to incorporate in your life activities and practices that are supportive to the environment no matter how insignificant these may appear.

5) Know that what is healthy for the environment is healthy for you. What is not healthy for the environment, no matter what the short-term gains may be, will ultimately threaten your own personal health, and the health of your children.

6) Study the lives and works of great naturalists, such as St. Francis of Assisi, Henry David Thoreau, and John Muir, to begin to appreciate the joy and spiritual fulfilment to be found in attuning yourself with nature.

7) Form environmental action associations, or the like, in order to raise the collective consciousness about the environment and to promote positive environmental action with a spiritual foundation.[2]

We should also mention in this context the work of theologians within the field of process theology,

---

[2] Rossi, Vincent. "The Eleventh Commandment: Toward an ethic of ecology." *Epiphany* 1 (1981: 2-18).

inspired by the process philosophy of Whitehead. They have been working out their own version of creation theology, which, although nominally inspired by Christian theology, departs considerably from present orthodoxies. Charles Hartshorne and John Cobb are in the forefront of this school of thought. The work of theological reconstruction is not limited to professional theologians only. The fruitful cooperative between the biologist Charles Birch and the theologian John Cobb brought us a wonderful volume entitled *The Liberation of Life* (1981), in which they argue that

> Life as the central symbol is God. ... Perhaps some who do not believe in what they understand by God may be willing to consider the appropriateness of faith in life. And perhaps others, who are quick to say that what is not absolutely controlling cannot be God, may be willing to recognize that it may yet be life. (p. 195)

The 'Theology of Earth' of Birch and Cobb and Eco-theology go hand in hand; and so much so, that some of our statements are almost interchangeable. I could not but subscribe totally under the following set of statements by Birch and Cobb:

> The dominant paradigms of the recent past have not expressed life, they have even attempted to explain life in terms of what is not alive. The liberation of thought about life from these lifeless

forms can help to liberate life all over the planet from the present deadening policies. That is why this book is called The Liberation of Life. It is not optimistic because it does not underestimate the power of death in established patterns of thought, economics, agriculture, family life, energy production, transportation and urban development. There is enormous potential for death in a global commitment to nuclear energy with its attendant problems of proliferation of nuclear armaments. It is easy to understand why people become despondent at the enormity of the political and economic problems of a divided world bent on pursuing clever means to no clear end.

But Life has strategies still untried and therein lies hope. To trust Life is to be sensitive to the possibilities it offers. It is to be receptive to Life's values ever pressing in on us from all sides and only blocked by us. It is to be open to the compassionate and tender response and to follow one's intuitions. Trust in Life releases human energy that makes it possible to transcend life as it is in order to make life as it could be.

Faith in Life's power to renew life exposes exploitation and injustice as denials of life. It calls for revolutionary commitment against them. But unless that struggle goes hand in hand with actual liberation there is no liberation in the struggle. Otherwise liberation movements take the stamp of their opponents in their struggle. Even when they succeed, they can lead to new oppressions and new alienations.

The greatest power in the world is the power that comes from faith in Life and the ideas this faith brings. The need now is for the critical ideas, the new impulses and the new enthusiasm whose time has come. (p. 330)

The search for new religious bearings is not limited to the Western world and the Christian culture. This search can be seen the world over. Religion is a most mysterious aspect of man's being. So often it is found oppressive, a kind of prison which we are impatient to leave. When we find ourselves outside this 'prison,' we also find that something is missing. Thus we cannot live with religion, and we cannot live without one. It is obvious, in our times, that traditional religions have exhausted their creative substance. This is true of not only Christianity.

In March 1984, I entertained a visitor from Japan, Professor Hiromasa Mase from Keio University in Tokyo, who is deeply concerned with Eco-philosophy and the future of religion. From my various conversations with him, and particularly from seminars he gave at the University of Michigan, a strange thing has transpired. While my students were adamant that Christianity has lost touch with the people, is no longer viable, is a ritualistic set of dogmas, more a preaching venue than a path of enlightenment and a vessel to behold our wholeness, Hiromasa Mase insisted that Christianity is still viable and can be reconstructed, particularly as it is capable of reflecting upon itself and criticizing itself—especially in such branches as process-theology. Thus, in the long run, it may reconstruct itself through its own effort.

The background of these discussions is significant. We, Westerners, have experienced the constraining perspectives and practices of Christianity and decided—in our hearts, at least—that the present churches are beyond mending. They are too tied to past dogmas, to the rather cruel conception of Christianity: "Christ died on the cross for your sins, remember, remember!" So we are quite inclined to take our clue and inspiration from Buddhism, its gentle path of compassion, its reverence for the Buddha in the blade of grass. On the other side was Professor Mase, who came from the Buddhist background, and found present Buddhism too quietistic, too immobile, too frozen in its past molds, unable to reflect upon itself, unable to be self-critical in its attempt to update itself to present realities.

Thus the situation was extraordinary. Far from being chauvinistic about our respective religions, we, from our Christian background, were leaning toward Buddhism, or at least saw in Buddhism more promise for the future than in Christianity. Hiromasa Mase, coming from the Buddhist background, saw in Christianity more promise for the future than in Buddhism.

This must be *signum temporis*. As we see the exhaustion of our own religion, we reach out to the other side. Of the great sayings coming from our Christian heritage, the simplest and the most profound of all is that "one does not live by bread alone".[3] We cannot live without any religion. We have been reaching out to find sustenance on the other side, in those great spiritual metaphors which have nourished the people of the Orient. As the result, while we still nominally call ourselves 'Christians,' we have been significantly changing our ways, at least those of us who care about our own spiritual life. The influence of Buddhism, although subtle and diffused, has been profound. The idea of the Buddha in the blade of grass, and in the motorcycle engine (*Zen and the Art of Motorcycle Maintenance*)[4] are no longer strange to us.

Buddhism will subtly pervade the Christian culture as it has pervaded Hinduism. The great Hindu philosopher and spiritual thinker Shankara (9th century AD) set as his goal to contain the spread of Buddhism in India. He crusaded for the return of Hinduism. On the surface, he succeeded. The vestiges of Hinduism and the caste system returned. But the subtle influence of Buddhism has remained, and has been all-pervading in Hindu culture. In the future, we shall evolve in the West the idea of the Jesus of the Cosmos as we quietly drop the idea of the Jesus of Nazareth. And perhaps one day we shall contemplate the image of Jesus and of the Buddha as two aspects of the same god...until we dissolve this image in another—the-god-in-becoming, in us.

The reconciliation of Christianity with Eco-theology,

---

3 Deuteronomy 8:3, and Matthew 4:4.

4 Book by Robert Pirsig (1974).

and perhaps with Buddhism, will not happened as the result of edicts solemnly proclaimed by some Vatican synods. It will happen as the result of creative acts of living. Through the transformation of our own consciousness, we shall live the new path, the spiritual Tao in which traditional symbols of Judaism and Christianity will be transformed into a new religious reality—evolving as our minds and reality do. We shall therefore be worshipping the creator by making more and more of his creature. The true worship of God will be a demonstration that we are in the image of God. And so much so that we shall be—becoming God.

"In truth, who knows god becomes god" (Mundaka Upanishad). As we become spiritually more and more evolved, we shall know God more and more—by being more and more acquainted with godliness in ourselves.

CHAPTER 10

HOME AS A SACRED ENCLOSURE

ECO-THEOLOGY is a restatement of our spiritual condition in the evolving universe which is home for mankind, for it is this universe which has engendered, nursed, and nurtured spiritual qualities which eventually made our *Oikos*—Greek for 'home'—sacred. *Theos* then is the highest quality of our existence as lived in the *Oikos*: our own home, nature, ecological habitats, the cosmos surrounding us. When our home becomes a sacred enclosure, *Oikos* and *Theos* are united, are fused together, and aspects of each other.

Eco-theology is the recognition of the process of the divinizing of the cosmos, whereby evolution has brought about spiritual qualities and has created the sacred ground for us so that our *Oikos* is both a dwelling and a temple. And our responsibility is to take care of our *Oikos*, both in the immediate boundaries of our home, and in its outer boundaries of the universe which has nurtured us.

Eco-theology provides an eschatological skeleton for remaking our concept of God in this universe, in this *Oikos*; and for redefining divinity in the human person.

Eco-theology provides a new coherence between evolution and theology; between physics and religion; between the existential and the cosmic in us. It spells out a new human liberation based on creativity, responsibility, and self-reliance, all of which are rooted in the notion of the self-creative character of the universe, of which we, as God-in-the-making, are a part. Eco-theology spells out a new meaning of humanness in us which is neither rooted in the old fashion humanism: "Man is the measure of all things" (Protagoras) or "The root of man is man himself" (Marx); nor is man reduced to old theological schemes, being nothing but a speck of dust against the infinity of God (or against the infinity of the physical universe— Newtonian Physics), but the new meaning derives from the image of HUMANITY-AS-MIND-MAKING, and co-creating the universe in the process.

We are *meaning makers*. We ascribe the meaning to the cosmos. In this sense, we are *cosmos makers*. Because we are meaning makers, we are cosmos makers. Because we are cosmos makers, we are meaning makers. We are neither God nor beasts but only the median in between. By creating fragments of Grace within ourselves, we move from beasts toward the other end. Creating fragments of Grace—this is all we are capable of. Not to create these fragments of Grace is to betray our Divinity, our Humanity.

Eco-theology promises to be ecumenical in the broadest sense. It accommodates not only the variety of Christian religions but opens its folds to other religions as well. We are all children of evolution. Through the evolutionary articulation we, as the human race, have splintered into various cultures and religions. Now on a new evolutionary level of articulation, we see the underlying unity: the sanctity of all creation, the same deep spiritual aspirations of all people who want to be fulfilled on all levels of their being; the same desire on the part of all people to be co-makers of their destiny and not only recipients of dogmas which make their life sterile, the same urge for wholeness which is ultimately a religious urge.

Eco-theology provides a new paradigm for wholeness; and, through symbiotic relationships with others, contributes to the wholeness of the entire earthly family. Unless we achieve wholeness through our own effort, no one can bestow this wholeness on us. We are living in the universe of Karma—as you sow, so you will reap—and not in the universe of revelation and miraculous salvation through the effort of others.

Wholeness is reaching out to the transcendental heaven, to the sacred, while our feet are firmly on the ground, and our own person is in the service of others. Wholeness is this peace within which connects us with the sacred but at the same time attunes us perfectly to our own body. Thus the existential and the theological become one within Eco-theology.

Saving the planet is no longer an environmental issue; it is a theological issue of first magnitude. If a nuclear holocaust happens, there will be no more souls to save. We thus witness the shift of the vision from the Jesus of Nazareth to the Jesus of the Cosmos.

Ecology and Christianity will be fused together, for each is too important for our well-being to be left out. The image of God of the Old Testament was born of concerns and problems different from ours. As our consciousness has changed—guided by new concerns and visions, of the interconnected and ecologically-viable cosmos—so has changed our image of God, and thus the reality of God. The vacant place of the supreme authority over the supersensory world, of which Nietzsche and Heidegger speak, cannot remain empty forever. We have discovered that this place is not a reality external to us—though we often think about it in this way—but a reality of our inner selves. As we cannot live without our inner selves, so we cannot live without the reality of God. The mysteries of human existence are endless.

At present, the reconciliation of traditional Christianity with Eco-theology, and other forms of new radical theology, seems difficult, if not impossible. Yet when we look at Christianity from the perspective of 3000 AD, we see it vastly changed! We are part of this change. We will find traditional religion, and specifically Christianity, adaptable to these vast changes, if only because we shall make Christianity so adaptable. Our evolutionary mind—which is God-in-the-making—is extremely adaptable. It will make traditional religion adaptable.

We have to have the courage *to be*, and the courage *to become*. We have to have the courage of joy; and the courage to cry; and the courage of our despair when things are temporarily out of joint. We have to have the courage to embrace others when they are in despair. Courage and hope are among the most important of our human attributes—they are the pre-condition of everything else.

As we put our Logos in a new order, so we put our mind in a new order; and so we create a new vehicle for our practical life. For practical life is but a dream happening while we are awake, a dream which, like music, follows a score composed by the mind. As mind commands, so we behave.

From the abyss of nothingness, we have emerged. It is not our destiny to return there. We must create new forms of light. *For we are light transforming itself.* We are photons transformed into the segments of grace.

As our condition changes from an amoeba to sentient beings, we enlarge our consciousness. As we enlarge our consciousness, we reach upward toward self-consciousness. As we acquire self-consciousness, we reach for understanding. As we reach for understanding, we reach for meaning. As we reach for meaning, we reach for grace. As we reach for grace, we reach for God. All is natural, and in a sense inevitable—when evolution creates the mind that becomes a source of light.

CHAPTER 11

THE NEW GOSPEL

The World is a Sanctuary. The world is not a machine but an exquisite sanctuary. To treat yourself well, to treat others well, you must know that the world is not a heap of meaningless rubbish but a place reverberating with divine energies. The world is a sanctuary.

You need to be one with the world. You need to realize that you are not an accident in this world. You need to realize that the world is not an accident either. You need to celebrate your own uniqueness in the world that is sacred. The sacredness of the world, your dignity and your sovereignty, are assured by the assumption that the world is a sanctuary.

The universe conceived as a sanctuary gives you the comfort of knowing that you live in a caring, spiritual place, that the universe has meaning and your life has meaning. To act in the world as a sanctuary is to make it reverential and sacred; and it is to make yourself elevated and meaningful. What the universe becomes depends on you. Treat it like a machine and it becomes a machine. Treat it like a divine place and it becomes a divine place. Treat it indifferently and ruthlessly and it becomes an indifferent and ruthless place. Treat it with love and care and it becomes a loving and caring place.

You were born creative. This is part of your likeness to God. Your creative nature is your gate to freedom. Be freer by consuming less. It is not right that you should be a slave manipulated by others who want you to be less critical and less creative, so that you consume more. As the spider reaches the liberty of space by means of its own thread, so the thinking person reaches freedom by means of the renunciation of unnecessary consumption.

You hold Destiny in your hands. Not only your own but the destiny of those with whom you are interlinked. You hold the future of the planet in your hands—the beautiful Gaia, to which you owe so much. You hold God's entire creation in your hands. We are not only God's children. We are his messengers, his shepherds, his co-workers. You co-create with God. This is why God gave you intelligence. This is why God made you creative. You safeguard God's law by not letting others spoil or destroy God's beautiful planet. Be truly creative by understanding that God wants you to co-create with him, that God wants you to protect creation which is the source of all creative powers.

You have the responsibility to do your part. Yes, you personally. You cannot hide forever by blaming the system, the industry, the bad people, the bigness of it all. You are an intelligent person in this world. This world will be renewed by intelligent people like you. You have always known that you have the responsibility. Now is the time to exercise it. You have always known that consumption is a trap and does not make you truly happy. You have always known that you have the spiritual potential within you which may be called upon one day. Now is the time to release this spiritual potential. Now is the time to fulfil your obligations to yourself, to others, to God. Yes, the greater the responsibility you assume, the more God is delighted with you. If you do nothing or close yourself in the shell of your egotism, you are of no use to anybody, you are of no use to God. To be truly happy you must accept your share of responsibility. The greater the share of responsibility you take, the greater person you become, the closer you come to God. Look at Mother Teresa, look at Gandhi—such simple people. Such magnificent people. So blessed by God. Why? Because they embraced the responsibility for all. They burned with their responsibility like a torch. But not in self-sacrifice—in the deepest self-fulfillment. To the glowing delight of God.

The web of life includes all forms of life, human and non-human. St. Francis speaks of our sister river, our brother fire, and Sir Brother Sun. All living beings, the foxes, the ravens, the wolves, and the deer were included in his family. And so they should be included in our family. Know thy place in the web of life. It is your nourisher, your sustainer, your family. You are surrounded by countless brothers and sisters in creation on whom you depend so vitally. Life is all-inclusive. And so our spirituality and our religion must be. It must include all forms of spiritual life. It must be tolerant to different images of God. Different spiritualities and different images of God are all branches of the divine tree. Let us forgo what divides us in our spiritual traditions. Let us cultivate what unites us. What unites us is the love of life, the love of this beautiful planet, the love of the magnificent universe which has begotten the planet and then us as a part of its divine flowering. Ecology is what unites us all. Ecological faith is what expresses our deepest bond to the planet Earth and to God who created it all. Let us not worship new gods. But let us worship the God of compassion, justice, and of ecological piety as he wants us to help him to reconstruct and heal the planet.

Be compassionate to others. Consume less so that others can simply survive. We now know that we live in one interconnected net. What we do in our corner of the net vitally affects what happens in other regions of the net. If we consume too much, use too much energy, produce too much waste, this will affect other weaker people, in other parts of the globe, who will be forced to sell their raw materials and to whom we will export our waste. This waste will return to us later. It will find its way to the food chain—and we will eat our poison—as we import food from other people.

We cannot live in peace on this planet until we have justice—justice not only for a select few, but for all people and for all creation. In the name of justice—human justice and God's justice—be frugal and compassionate. Help the planet, help other people by demanding less, consuming less—while you become a more spiritual person. The more you consume, the less spiritually attuned you become. The more spiritually attuned you are, the more mindful, the more compassionate, the more frugal you become; and therefore more just. Frugality and justice are firmly connected nowadays. God calls you to render his justice by being radiantly frugal. Frugality is grace without waste.

Be gentle to yourself. You have endured enough stresses and unnecessary battering. You are tough. You can take a lot. But by taking too much, your heart hardens too much. You must have a gentle heart so that you behold yourself and others compassionately. Holding destiny in your hands means beholding yourself and others compassionately.

Be mindful how you treat your body. Don't abuse it. It is God's gift. Treat it as such. If you overeat constantly, it is not good for your health. You are then careless about your divine gift. Besides, the food that you overconsume is probably taken from the mouths of those who will go to sleep hungry tonight. Golden medium is our path. This is what great spiritual traditions recommend: neither excessive austerities nor excessive indulgence. On the wall of one of the Franciscan monasteries we read: "What you have and you don't need is stolen from those who need it and don't have it." Does this sound too radical for you? Then think again and think deeper. Maybe you will hear the ring of truth.

Be mindful of what you think. If there is too much rubbish in your head, then there is no room for God in it.

It is said in a sacred scripture: "If men thought of God as much as they think of the world, who would not attain liberation?" That is one of the cosmic laws. Keep the mind pure, for what a person thinks, he becomes. How much time do you allow yourself to dwell in the space of God? You claim to have no time. You claim that there is too much pressure on you. But these are the excuses for not attending to what is vitally important to you. You can find time to talk to your inner self. And then God will speak to you. Those who do not have time for their inner selves, God ignores. Speak more often to God and less often to the television. You will then find yourself in the space of peace.

You were born into a beautiful world. Yes, the world is scarred, but still beautiful. The morning dew on the blades of grass in early June, the smell of hay after the grass has been cut and is contentedly drying, the darkness of a big forest confiding to you its mysteries, the joyous clouds playing in the high stratosphere to make you light and joyous, are all signs of the beauty of the visible world.

We have spoiled a great deal of this beautiful world. The rivers that were once so clean that you could not only swim in them but also drink from them have become dirty pools. But not all is lost. We can renew what we have spoiled. We can bring back radiance to the earth. We can clean polluted skies, polluted lands, our polluted minds. We can do it if we remember what an incredible creation the earth has been; what an incredible creation we ourselves are! We have the will and the energy to do it—if we have the vision. Let us put our wills together to bring back radiance to this incredible world so that the earth is good and fair again.

Your nature is divine. The whole visible world around you is divine. The miracle of a magnificent oak tree growing out of a humble acorn is incredible. The whole universe is divine in its forms. You stand in front of an unending glory of continuous creation in which all the divine forms sing and dance to enchant and delight you. Remove the scales from your eyes so that you can see.

You are more aware of your divinity than the crab or the oak tree. Hence your responsibility is so much greater. Celebrate your divinity on behalf of those forms which are less conscious. How do you celebrate? By being responsible, by being reverential, by beholding yourself as a sacred particle in the sacred universe. When you are awakened from the stupor of unseeing, you are bound to embrace this divine cosmos with joy. For this divine cosmos is meant for joy and celebration. We do not live in a valley of misery and tears. Celebrate by renewing the Earth, by renewing yourself, by paying homage to God—while co-creating with him.

Your divinity must reveal itself in your action. Allow your inner voice to speak. And follow it. Link yourself with the highest light and become it. Don't be ashamed of your dignity and greatness. Being human, you are great. Being divine, you are great. Don't allow yourself to be cheapened or trivialized by consumerism and ordinary stupidities. Being trivial or cheap is not your destiny. This is not what you want to be. This is not

God's plan for you. God's plan and Your Inner Voice are one. Listen to both attentively. And don't be afraid of being human—thus divine. You need to fulfil your inner mission, your divine potential.

Suffering cannot be avoided. Suffering should be diminished and reduced as far as possible. But suffering cannot be avoided. It is part of our human world—just as joy is part of our human world. And there is a time for each.

Through suffering you learn your humanity. Through suffering you learn compassion, which enables you to understand the suffering of others. Through suffering you learn wisdom. You cannot live meaningfully in this world without some wisdom. You cannot acquire wisdom without some suffering. It is thus that we should consider suffering—as a teacher of wisdom and compassion, not of spurious pain. Those deep moments of solitude and suffering are necessary to make you a deeper person. Thus suffering is a cauldron in which your humanity acquires shape and makes itself divine. Those who have suffered a lot, understand a lot. They are the special children of God who went through many trials because they needed to learn much.

Would it not be better if, from the start, God had eliminated suffering altogether? This is not how this world works. It works through becoming. All forms of life mature through becoming. Going through the process of becoming includes suffering. For every becoming entails some pain. When the original acorn, which is about to become a mighty oak, splits up to give rise to a new tree, it suffers the pain of birth, the pain of becoming. Suffering and becoming, maturing and acquiring wisdom, are part of the same process of life. You cannot avoid the life process while you are alive. Thus you cannot avoid suffering. Embrace it gently, but without being too fond of it. Ultimately, suffering must be transcended in favor of the glowing radiance of life—of which we all partake.

The fact of death cannot be avoided. Lead your life in such a way that you can meet death with serenity and dignity. What is on the other side of the curtain is a mystery. Only on the other side will you know why you couldn't know what is there from this side.

You should not fear death. Your entire life should be a training for death. Leading life as a preparation for death makes your daily chores so much easier. You then have a perspective—how to look at things which are important and which are not. Remember, at some point you will need to leave behind all your possessions and all your earthly ties. You must be serene about this. Such is life. It continuously metamorphosizes itself in endless cycles. You belong to one cycle. But your energy will be circulated in the universe forever.

Celebrate! The universe is in a state of self-celebration. The universe is a place of suffering. Thus we were born to suffer. The universe is a place of celebration. Thus we were born to celebrate. Hence the inevitability of suffering and the inevitability of celebration. The Sufis, the Christian mystics, and other ecstatics know this truth well, namely, that the universe is for celebration!

It is easy to become overwhelmed by suffering. It is natural to recognize the suffering of others—as the bond that unites us. But there also exists another bond—the bond of ecstatic celebration which unites all the pulsating cosmos. Every living cell in the human organism, every bird in the sky and every tree in a healthy forest is singing the song of celebration. The greatness of the creator reveals itself in the fact that it created the universe which realizes itself through celebration. To acknowledge that the universe is in a state of perpetual celebration is to acknowledge its unspeakable grandeur, is to acknowledge the creative powers of God. True religion must be one which expresses and embodies this celebration—as we co-create with God and with the universe.

We are the glowing particles of the radiant universe. We are the cosmic dancers expressing the universe's ecstatic energy. We are the poets through whom the universe expresses its poetry. Through us the universe and God are singing their cantatas and fugues. The universe is a place of suffering. The universe is a place of celebration. One does not negate the other. Yet through celebration we redeem our suffering.

From Liberation to Enlightenment

What is your path of liberation? To begin with, you need to take yourself seriously. What does it mean to take yourself seriously? Certainly not to be a pompous ass, full of gas and self-importance. But equally certainly, not to become a cipher manipulated by others. To take yourself seriously is to attempt to realize your potential. Yes, intellectual potential. But also your ultimate potential. To realize your ultimate potential is to become a realized person and an enlightened being. You can never recapture your divinity if you never assume that you are divine.

To take yourself seriously is to aspire to become God—without hallucinations, without megalomania, without losing your balance; by following a sane path, which becomes a path of grace and ultimately the path of divinity. Yes, in your daily life you will find that you so often depart from the path by being bumped aside by external circumstance or your own indolence. The point is not to mortify yourself by crying, "Oh, I have failed again!" The point is to quietly return to the path. Center yourself. And keep going.

Be aware of the awesome beauty of the universe—as it unfolds through you. We are the divinity unfolding. There is hope. And there is a future—if we take ourselves seriously. We shall straighten up what is crooked. We shall purify and heal what is stained and polluted—if we take ourselves seriously, if we follow our divinity.

When can you hope to reach enlightenment? That depends how seriously you take yourself. In the meantime, you have the teaching of the Buddha, of Jesus, of Gandhi, of Krishnamurti, and yes, of Eco-philosophy.

Achieve wholeness through your own effort. Unless we achieve wholeness through our own effort, no one can bestow this wholeness on us. We are living in the universe of Karma—as you sow so you will reap; not in the universe of revelation and miraculous salvation through the effort of others. Wholeness is reaching out to the transcendental heaven, to the sacred, while your feet are firmly on the ground, and your own person is in the service of others. Wholeness is this peace within, which connects you with the sacred but at the same time attunes you perfectly to your own body. Thus the existential and the theological become one.

CHAPTER 12

ECOLOGICAL SPIRITUALITY

Spirituality is a sublime subject. Great minds and souls have reflected on it and left behind many illuminating insights. Yet we need to reflect on it again, if only because we wish to prove that we are spiritually alive. Our circumstances and problems are unprecedented and they require a new spiritual response, a new form of spirituality. Older spiritualities were created in response to different problems, within the context of a different worldview, and in order to articulate different dimensions of the human condition.

Spirituality is an articulated essence of the human condition of a given time. This conception of spirituality enables us to cherish various forms of spirituality in various cultures and religions; but also informs us that there isn't one form of spirituality for all times, for all people, for all the conditions of the human universe. As the world changes and unfolds, knowledge grows and unfolds, the human mind changes, the human psyche changes, the human condition is re-articulated, and thus human spirituality takes different forms.

In our times, we witness the dawn of the Ecological Perspective, or the ecological worldview. Within this perspective, the universe is viewed as a sanctuary. To act in the world as if it were a sanctuary is to make it reverential and sacred. What the universe becomes depends on you. Treat it like a machine and it becomes a machine. Treat it like a divine place and it becomes a divine place. Reverence for life, and for all there is in the universe, is the first condition of ecological spirituality. To celebrate the miracle of creation is to behold the world reverentially.

An in-depth comprehension of ecology is *reverence in action*, is a deep identification with the beauty of life pulsating through the universe until we become part of it. Thus understanding becomes empathy. Empathy becomes universal reverence. This reverence is a form of spirituality. In our times, the ecological and the spiritual become one.

To worship God in our times is to save the planet. If we lose the environment, we lose God. Healing the planet and healing ourselves is spiritual work of the first magnitude in our day and age. Whatever our race and religion, ecology binds us all together. Ecology is the universal religious project of our time. The idea of redemption acquires a new meaning—it means redeeming the world by healing the earth. We need to emphasize: healing the earth is the spiritual work of our time.

To understand religious devotion is to recognize that *all religions are forms of worship of the beauty and integrity of the planet.* The greening of world religions in our times is a clear indication that the call of the crying earth is heard by the churches.

Spirituality is also, and has always been, the realization of our inner potential, the actualization of the inner god within us. We need to treat each other according to what we can potentially become: divine lights uplifting ourselves and helping others to heal, to integrate, to become more reverential. Working on ourselves to release and articulate our inner divinity, and working in the outside world to heal the earth, are complementary aspects of ecological spirituality.

The waning of religious forms of spirituality does not absolve us from the responsibility of healing the earth, and from actualizing our spiritual potential. In spite of the religious crisis of our times, and perhaps because of it, we must have the courage to meet—in each of us individually—the savior of the Cosmos.

CHAPTER 13

THE KEY TO HAPPINESS

Do not strive for happiness. You can only arrive at happiness while striving for other things. Happiness is not a fixed state of being; it is a state of perpetual becoming. Happiness cannot be designed. When happiness arrives, you are no longer conscious of striving for it.

What should you strive for? For meaning in life, for the fulfilment that goes beyond your individual egoistic self. You are as great as the causes you aspire to. Great causes elevate you and make you transcend your small self. Great causes pervade you with reverence and infuse you with dignity, which are necessary components of a worthy life. Stretch yourself to the maximum in the service of others, in the cause of altruism. Merge with the larger scheme of things by understanding that human destiny is made of the stars and not only of ordinary clay. And then your life will be enhanced, your being enlarged. And perhaps as a byproduct, you will arrive at happiness.

What is happiness? The equilibrium of your being which is recognized by others as a state of serenity that is inspiring and uplifting; which is felt by you as a state of inner tranquility that gives you strength and determination; not a state of sensual satisfaction or a state of physical comfort, but a state of inner radiance which you will recognize more and more as you approach it closer and closer. Happiness is being at peace with yourself while the self is united with a larger order of things.

The truly blessed people, the giants of human thought and spirit, the Gandhis and the Schweitzers, did not search for happiness, yet we find their lives radiant and inspiring—full to the brim in the service of great causes, in the service of others, in the service of large ideals which alone make sense of human destinies.

CHAPTER 14

FROM ECO-THEOLOGY
TO A THEOLOGY OF LIGHT

Light Becoming God

God is Light. This intuition is acceptable to almost
everybody; even to people who at the same time cherish
other descriptions or deep intuition of God. Light as God
appears in many sacred scriptures. Since time
immemorial, human beings have been struck by the
extraordinary nature of Light—its luminosity and its all-
pervading nature. Eventually, Light was linked with
Being, which people later described as the highest. They
vested all the potency of Light in God. They forgot that
Light was only an inspiration to envisage God in the
image of Light.[1]

In the embrace of Light, all creation is sacred. God
smiles through the 'radiance' of Light because God is
this 'radiance' itself. What is the most beautiful in God is
the 'radiance' of Light; what is the most significant in
the image of God is the quality of Light; what is the most

---

[1] Perhaps the first articulation of this idea in history was by the Egyptian
pharaoh Akhenaten, circa 1350 BC. For one account of his life and his
philosophy of light, see *Son of God, Son of the Sun* by Savitri Devi (2015).

important in the works of God is the journey from darkness to the highest luminosity. In the nature of Light are embedded the most essential characteristics of God.

The idea of Light becoming God is appealing and intuitively simple. Yet the way towards the final stage of this metamorphosis has eluded us so far. Was Light born as God all of a sudden? Was it, perhaps, pregnant with 'God' and bore it, as children are born? Metaphorically speaking, it must have been pregnant with 'God.' It had to contain the potency of God so that this potency could be actualized at an appropriate time. The process of this actualization was subtle and mysterious and mind-boggling. The origin of God was bound to be mysterious. Actually, every new departure of cosmic evolution is a bit mysterious. As human consciousness matured and deepened, the sense emerged that there are things and phenomena existing beyond the realm of the tangible and the observable. There emerges the feeling that there exists a trans-physical world, which is mysterious and powerful.

Prehistoric humans began to intuit that the cosmos is a repository of immense powers. These powers reside in trees, in herbs, in animals, in the realms above. They all reside in human beings as well. Thus, the sense of the invisible forces surrounding humans haunted us for many thousands of years. Then slowly, and subtly, there emerged a sense of the sacred; a sense that these invisible forces affect human destinies, are responsible for their well-being—during and perhaps even after the present life. Human beings began to cultivate intimate relationships with these special forces. They acknowledged them by paying homage to them, through rituals, both individually and together as a community.

We should understand that the sensing of these special forces, and then establishing of special rituals linking human with the forces, could not have happened if the human consciousness was not keen enough and aware enough. And here is the essential point: What was not registered in the human consciousness could not have existed outside. Human consciousness had to become refined and articulate so that it could conceive and perceive in appropriate ways the transcendent aspects of reality. Without humans conceiving this transcendent reality, this reality could not have been experienced or apprehended in any way whatever.

Thus, the sense of transcendent reality emerged. Simultaneously, there emerged an awareness that we live in this reality, that we are a part of this reality. The state of our consciousness dictates what we can experience; what we can perceive, conceive and even imagine. So important it is, that with a slight exaggeration only, we can say that unless certain 'realities' are conceived by the human mind or human imagination, they cannot be manifested in the outer cosmos. This means that the process of discovery is not simply a process of 'uncovering', of what already exists there, but a process of co-creation with the cosmos and Light.

With the development of human consciousness, a delineation of the transcendent forces was attempted and accomplished. This very consciousness further led to the discovery/creation of the sphere of the sacred. Slowly but inexorably, a sense of spirituality was chiseled out. The images of icons, as beholding and emanating special powers, were conceived. The sense of deities, as an augmentation of these powers, was the inevitable outcome. It also brought about the creation of the transcendent realms where, it was believed, the gods resided.

In time, these gods became the focal points of transcendent power. They were acknowledged as controlling our lives. In due time, religions emerged. They became institutional structures of power. Their influence was vast and all-pervading. They were supposed to give us spiritual support in our individual and social lives. This they did, so often to our benefit. However, as time went on, they also turned out to be very controlling—then intimidating, and sometimes imprisoning.

Religions as Filters of Big Light

Monotheistic gods eventually declared themselves to be the source of all Light and all divinity. This is evident in Abrahamic religions and also in Hinduism. Brahman is the ground and the source of all there is—eternal, unchanging, perfect. And so is God Jehovah—among Abrahamic religions.

In these religions, there is an acute awareness of the importance of the spiritual sustenance for humans.

CHAPTER 14

Spirituality and divinity are the highest 'goods'. Against them, everything else pales into insignificance. The whole way of life is so organized as to elevate and enhance the concerns for spiritual well-being, and to diminish other concerns. The scope of various other religions is so different. Consequently, the forms of light, which are 'pre-selected and pre-arranged,' are also different. One is indeed puzzled. Why so many conceptions of God? Why so many different routes? Why this intense competition amongst religions? If God is one, there should not be so much rivalry and competition among religions.

We are often told that indeed God is *one*. Furthermore, that various religions are its different manifestations. On the surface this sounds plausible. But actually it does not explain anything. Why do religions try to destroy each other? Why all these confusions about the same God? We need answers, which are much deeper answers than traditionally given.

We should understand, to begin with, that none of the religions embrace the whole of Big Light or can access it. Each capture only a part of it. And it does so in a peculiar way, not directly but through some kinds of filters. Each religion, and each spiritual tradition, is a kind of filter through which the Big Light is filtered, processed, and transformed. The result of this filtering are specific teachings and precepts, characteristics of a given religious tradition.

Because these ideas are rather new, I shall allow myself to reiterate some main points. Now, because the filters of different religions are so different, religions are different. Each filter, if it is significantly specific, establishes a separate religion, establishes relationships with Light in a specific way. It is not the same relationship for all religions. Some of these filters overlap. Hence, the similarity of the various religious teachings. Some of these filters are considerably different. Hence considerable difference, among religions, including different conceptions of God or the Divine. Each filter is legitimate—insofar as it reaches for the Light. But none can be claimed to be the only true one.

Some religious traditions claim to be the only true ones. These are the most competitive ones. They usually are the main source of trouble—in the human world. They are prepared to go to war and exterminate others in the name of their truths. Actually most religious traditions are somewhat competitive. They jealously guard and uphold the superiority of their creed.

But some religions and spiritual traditions exhibit more tolerance than others and, at the same time, possess less of a competitive zeal. Among them are Taoism and Buddhism. They offer their teachings and leave you alone. They are like Light itself—forever giving, benignly, gently and peacefully, respecting you and your dignity.

One has to look very carefully at these divine filters, which we call religions. They can be very different. Big Light shines on all. It gives and gives. It never withdraws from giving. By its nature, it cannot be discriminating to some human beings because of their caste or gender. Only the filters are discriminating. Discrimination is the beginning of divisions; then of animosities and hatred; finally of persecution. This is not the way of the Big Light.

Existing religions are completely unable to explain why they quarrel with each other. They are unable to explain what the real differences between them are. They are at a loss to see that the same benevolent God can be an inspiration to religious wars.

The idea of religious 'filters' provides a clue to all these dilemmas. The power of the filters is camouflaged, really hidden. Ultimately, the filters are ingenious works of the human imagination. Their specific frame and configuration depend on the genius of the founder. The filters *in toto* represent the human genius in structuring the Big Light so that it becomes available, comprehensible, and inspiring to ordinary people.

These founders (of great religions) are messengers of the Big Light. They were aware that the Light they witnessed was extraordinary and as such they called it 'divine'. The new consciousness they possessed rendered the world sacred and divine.

The Way of Mysticism

Big Light and mysticism are intimately connected. Mysticism is a big enigma. And yet such a big invitation. We are afraid of it. And we are entranced by it. Who are the mystics? The living torches of the Big Light.

The mystics are both a pride of, and an embarrassment to, established religions. The religions want to appropriate the mystics. On the other hand, the churches fear them. Religions and churches are quite aware that what the mystics represent does not agree with the canons and dogmas established by them. Hence the embarrassment—and finally, attempts to suppress mystics as heretics.

Mystics defy all religions. Not that they do it consciously as an act of defiance. They go directly for Big Light. It is not because they intend to be defiant but because they seek the Big Light. They willfully connect with the Big Light and embrace it. Through their peculiar genius, they can connect with the Big Light and not be 'scorched' by it. To live in the continuous presence of the Big Light and be a constant witness to it, is a superhuman experience. In this sense, they are superhuman. What strikes us first of all is that they are so 'free'. The state of their being represents the ultimate dimension of freedom. They cannot be bound by anything. Their freedom is so beautiful. Yet, a bit terrifying. Nothing binds them; but nothing ever supports them, except the Big Light.

The way of mysticism is hard to define. It is a pathless path. Thus we cannot fully understand it, if at all. We cannot learn it. We cannot follow it, as there are no tracks to follow, and we cannot learn it, as there is nothing to learn. We can speak about it, we can read about it, we can write about it. But our words are like straw in the wind— a bit deceitful. The more coherent the description, the more surely it misses the meaning and depth of mysticism. There are no adequate 'statements' which could faithfully describe the nature of mysticism.

The mystic signifies the ecstasy of being—this overwhelming Light which penetrates and emanates from the overwhelming radiance that penetrates his soul; the sense of total tranquility and joy; and the rapture of being. He signifies the sense of touching the Divine or being touched by the Divine; the sense of being close to God...yet, be wary of words! Words so easily fit us into conventional idioms; nay, force us into conventional religious language. And this language claims that mysticism is an experience of God (with the hidden premise that this is the God of the given religion). The problem is that every religion wants to see the mystic experience as the manifestation of *its* god; and not of any other god; not of the cosmic god, not of the Big Light.

The established religions have far-reaching tentacles. They claim to be the sole vehicle for interpreting spiritual phenomena. They interpret mystical experience as a peculiar form of communion with God—according to their understanding of God and according to the precepts of their religion. Those who have undergone a deep mystical experience can testify that they did not encounter any particular god but a great Light. A mystical experience can be interpreted *a posteriori* as an experience of a particular God (whatever its name). It is a unique and subjective experience. Later, established religions try to affix their interpretations and impose their seals of approval.

In many aboriginal tribes, mystic states have been known. Sometimes they were induced through hallucinogenic drugs, through ecstatic dancing, or continuous singing for days. This was usually an attempt to merge with the Ultimate Reality. Amongst them the shamans, the seers, and the medicine men were the people who were sensitive to the Great Spirit or Big Light. In their practices they consciously sought unity with Big Light, or whatever name they used for the Ultimate.

There are paths to the Big Light which are beyond the organized religions. The great mystics are not trapped by religions; rather, they seek to meet with Big Light. The trouble starts when they try to explain the experience of Big Light in the language accepted within a given religion. One cannot 'describe' Big Light. The experience of Big Light is ecstatic. It borders on madness. Some went beyond the line, never to return. The Big Light devoured them. The best explanation of the mystic experience is silence—the great silence of the mystic who knows but is unable to describe. And the great silence on our part which enables us to understand even without words.

Mysticism, as a historical phenomenon, undeniably proves that the Big Light exists and that it is accessible to all; although more to some than to others. By its extraordinary nature, mysticism is fascinating. It gives us insights into our deepest nature. Deep down we long for it. Yet, the rational mind often tells us to hold back. It whispers to us that mysticism is beyond us—and thus removes us from the mystic joy.

Mysticism exists in all cultures. It is not a phenomenon or a property of any religion. It is a cosmic phenomenon. It is a challenge to those who have not been able to face it and also an invitation to the people who have been initiated. We recognize the philosopher by his theories; the mystic by his glow. Had it not been for his glowing self, we would have understood the mystic to be merely knowledgeable. He would have been rather like a philosopher. It is paradoxical; the less the mystic says, the better his expression.

Light is the kernel of mystical experience; then it can be conveyed by words, which are Light themselves. Here are some examples:

"Light is visible by Light. The *nous* sees itself, and this light, shining on the soul, enlightening it and makes it a member of the spiritual world."
— Plotinus, *Enneads*, V.3.8

"Light rare, untellable, lighting the very light."
— Walt Whitman, "Prayer of Columbus"

"I saw Eternity the other night like a great ring of pure and endless light."
— Henry Vaughan, "The World"

"He who knows the truth knows that Light, and he who knows that Light knows Eternity."
— St Augustine, *Confessions*, VII.10

The Ethics of Light

This discussion has already amply demonstrated what an extraordinary phenomenon Light is! When its deepest meaning is grasped, then it can be clearly understood: why religions quarrel with each other; why they are incomplete; why they cannot understand the meaning of mysticism and often attempt to suppress it.

The understanding of the deep nature of Light enables us to comprehend realms which are important, but which have languished in obscurity. Among these phenomena is 'human ethics' and 'human freedom'. Yes, we are acquainted with them. Yet, we need to re-examine them in order to see that they are part of the theology of Light in the broad sense: they derive their deeper meaning from the very nature of Light. I shall attempt to show that a new ethics, of a truly universal nature, can be derived from the ethics of Light itself. I shall also argue that the meaning of human freedom is contained in the meaning of the freedom of Light. Let me discuss ethics first.

The fundamental nature of Light is to always give. It is always glowing and illuminating; illuminating and nourishing; nourishing and uplifting; uplifting and transforming. Such is the nature of Light. Its very nature is abundance. It showers the earth with energy, which is the source of all. Its inexhaustible generosity has embraced humankind too. We are saturated with abundance. We are truly living in the universe of abundance.

It is time to become aware of that. We are beings of Light. In our ethics, we must mirror the elan of light. The elan with which Light unfolds is reflective of its giving, generous, and transcending nature. Our ethics must be congruent with the laws of the cosmos. These laws, in one way or another, recapitulate the thrust and elan of light unfolding.

We are therefore postulating human ethics, which accepts and embodies the elan of the abundance of Light. Light is always giving. Thus human ethics must be based on giving and not hoarding. From the imperative of abundance follows the imperative of giving and generosity.

Other ethical principles which are latent in the nature of Light, and which must become principles of human ethics are: sharing, solidarity, and love. Furthermore, the ethics of Light must include: harmony, transcendence, spiritual well-being, and beauty. Why harmony? Because generosity and sharing are meant to benefit the overall harmony. Why transcendence? Because the overall harmony is not one of immediate satisfaction but a transcendent quest for spiritual self-realization.

Here, then, are eight principles of the ethics of Light:

- Giving
- Generosity
- Sharing
- Solidarity
- Love

- Harmony
- Transcendence
- Spiritual quest

The ethics of Light, which we are postulating here, are based on a deeper reading of the structure of the cosmos. For this reason, we may call it a *cosmic ethics*. This ethics is natural, intuitive, and rational. It is not based on any religion or divine revelation. Yet, we can call it divine because of the overall divinity of the unfolding of light, which these ethics embody and reflect. This is an altruistic ethics because all beings in the Universe cooperate with each other. It cannot be otherwise in the Universe derived from Light and governed by Light's laws.

At this point, the imperative of altruism, the necessity and viability of altruism, is as compellingly explained as it ever can be: We are altruistic because we are cosmic beings, because Light in us inspires us and compels us to continue its journey—of giving and sharing.

Altruistic ethics is part of the cosmic law. As we begin to understand the deeper structure of the Universe, we begin to accept that the higher we go, the more we share with other beings; thus we give more and more—because we are inwardly impelled to give, otherwise we slide towards decay. The altruistic ethics of Light is part of its spirituality because it is part of the divine vehicle of life, and of spirit evolving to ever-new heights.

This sense of giving and sharing is particularly apparent in illustrious beings, such as Jesus and the

Buddha. They have been giving and giving. Indeed, they have been giving not only kindness, love, and compassion, but invariably Light. For the highest qualities of human behavior—love, divinity, compassion and kindness—reside in the womb of Light. They are themselves expressions and manifestations of Light. Those who are considered the greatest human beings are recognized as the shining light.

Light will prevail because it must, because of its fundamental nature. Its very nature is giving and giving. It showers the whole cosmos with its abundance. When we reflect on this, we realize that the Universe is in good shape. We are in good shape. The future of humanity is in a good shape.

Light as Freedom

Searching for the meaning of Light among the items of the physical universe is a futile endeavor. Light is about one fantastic freedom, which unveils itself to us when we recognize the true nature of Light, and our place in the unfolding 'tapestry of Light'.

Light creates freedom at every point of its creativity. For every creative act is born out of freedom. To be true vehicles and repositories of Light, we must embody this extraordinary freedom of Light with which it acts. It moves and dances in freedom and with freedom. This freedom exceeds any freedom known to humans. This freedom of Light is so intoxicating, so overwhelming, so embracing that even thinking of it makes us free, makes us realize what strange and wonderful beings we are—moving along the paths of Light's freedom. Of all the forms of liberation, the liberation through Light is most profound. All forms of freedom are concealed expressions of the freedom of Light. All the virtues and qualities we possess somehow reflect the glories of Light.

Light is freedom. Confinement is the denial of Light. An enlargement of Light in us brings about an enlargement of our being and freedom. We simply are unaware what great freedoms are available within our psyche and spirit. Only great artists, from time to time, have the courage to embrace these resources of freedom.

Freedom is such an important gift of spiritual liberation. And such an important criterion of the worth of Light itself. Another name for Big Light is Big Freedom. It requires inner strength, the strength of our character to search for inner light and for spiritual destiny. In seeking spiritual freedom, we often need to extricate ourselves from the religious matrix, which has defined us hitherto. Our identity and this matrix are often intertwined and interwoven. Thus we must be careful so that our identity does not collapse during the process of freeing ourselves from the old (religious) matrix and all its trappings. Therefore we must be strong. It is an abortive quest for spiritual liberation if, instead of finding new spiritual nourishment, we land in a fundamentalist confinement, or worse still, we slip into nihilism and total relativism. Nihilism and relativism bring no freedom. They bring confinement.

CHAPTER 14

Now, religions which imprison and manipulate their followers are not true religions of Light. A true religion enlarges and deepens your freedom. It gives you wings and does not bring chains. The greatest freedom of Light is its capacity to metamorphosize itself into the divine substance, which some call God. The greatest freedom of human beings is of the same kind. It is the capacity to metamorphosize themselves into celestial beings, by incorporating the highest attributes of Light. This freedom of Light is so divine that we can hardly find words to describe it. When we contemplate this kind of freedom, we are inclined to think that everything is possible. We feel God-like; which we are. Light is all-embracing. Light is all-creative. Light is quintessentially free. But Light is not perfect. The creative process is not perfect. It is so because whatever is creative, is open and undetermined. Creativity signifies continuous transcendence. He who creates, makes mistakes. Creative mistakes are not faulty endeavors. They are attempts to open reality in new ways. This is what the true meaning of transcendence is. By creative mistakes, human beings learn. In this endeavor, they follow the modus of Light. Light is a continuous learner. And so is evolution. And so is all life.

Monotheistic gods are supposed to be perfect. If they are, therefore, they are uncreative and stagnant. Remember: *creativity means transcendence*. Transcendence always includes searches and some mistakes. There is no perfect way to transcend. Transcendence means groping towards the new amidst uncertainty. Uncertainty means stumbling and trying. All creative endeavors are of this kind. Transcendence simply means going beyond amidst freedom, creativity, and error. This is the way of Light. And of humans—who have inherited freedom and creativity of Light.

Light signifies the greatest freedom imaginable. Traditional gods are antiquated and petrified. Past religions have mainly exploited us. They have been the instruments of suppression. They have been our tethers. Light is Liberation! We have spent too much time in the stone-age and acquired too much of the stone-age mentality. We have spent enough time in caves. And we acquired more than enough of the cave mentality. The time has come to leave the caves and the mentality of slaves in the caves. The time has come to emerge into the lucid Light and embrace the wisdom of Light and the freedom of Light. Light is not accidental to our freedom. It is essential to it. Light is the bringer of our freedom. Freedom is a form of Light; it is this essential modality through which our most essential human attainments can be realized and safeguarded. Freedom, in the deepest sense, is spiritual freedom, connected with the aspiration to be Divine.

The Theology of Light

Big Light is more encompassing than any religion and all religions. Religions are only bridges. Light is more primary, more powerful, more elementary. Light is the primary source of all, including all religions, prophets, and divinities of various religions. Light informs us that the Buddha was not Light itself, but a reflection of the Ultimate Light, a high embodiment of Light. For the same reason, Jesus was not Light itself, but a reflection of the Ultimate Light. And the same holds for Lao Tzu and other Illumined Ones.

Therefore, we cannot claim that Jesus was the highest Light, while what was before was an obscure light; and that what was after was a distorted light—although shining with some background light. There have been some attempts to subsume and incorporate the theology of Light into existing religions, specifically, Christian theology. By understanding the nature of existing religions as monopolies, such attempts are not surprising. But they are illegitimate. We do not want to go backwards. We have shown that all religions are derived from Light. The ultimate source is Light. The primacy of the divinity of Light is unquestioned and stupendously clear. To claim that Jesus is the Ultimate Light would simply mean to undermine the foundations of the theology of Light and transform it into Christian theology. The theology of Light has transcended Christian theology.

This is not an attack on Christianity. Far from it. By accepting the primacy of Light—Light as the source—we can easily follow the teaching of Jesus, that is, what is most essential in the teachings proposed by Jesus Himself. In actual fact, the ethics of love, so important to the Gospel of Jesus, reflects and embodies the ethics of Light more closely than any other ethics proposed by spiritual prophets—with the exception of the Buddha, perhaps.

Indeed, these two spiritual giants, Jesus and the Buddha, understood the meaning of Light most profoundly.

People must not be nervous about their own spiritual traditions. Light is not competing with any of them. It only provides a large comfortable platform on which they all can be accommodated. Light has existed for several billion years. Organized religions have existed for merely three millennia. It should not be surprising that Light can be a host to relative new-comers.

I have mentioned the idea of the theology of Light. What is then the theology of Light? It is a new vision: A new holistic vision of all there is. Expressed in the simplest way: theology of Light is this vision, which informs us that there is one stupendous unity in the Universe, which stems from Light and is nursed and nurtured by Light. It is a vision of unity amidst the relentless creativity. This unending creativity is of such power that it verges on the Divine. Nay, this creative unity is Divine. Our theology of Light is thus based on three main pillars: *unity, creativity, divinity.*

Everything else flows from it. The creativity of the cosmos or of Light is so powerful that it could bring out divinities, gods, and religions from the original womb of Light. This unitary phenomenon of Light, which possesses such enormous powers, should not frighten but delight us. For we are part of this unity, part of this creativity, and part of this divinity. Moreover, our creative and divine mind could conceive of it and justify it.

What I have described is not a theoretical scheme or a theological fantasy, but a powerful matrix, which involves a new altruistic ethics—it has enormous positive consequences for human kind and for all creation; as well as a new sense of freedom, which is so liberating and so empowering; as well as other strategies for human action, which can be applied in real life for the benefit of all. The matrix proposed invites us all to a holy interaction for which we have long awaited. The dream of a fair world is not a fantasy but a possibility. It is a promise of Light, which Light can deliver. But only with our help.

The journey of Light is the most stupendous of all journeys. We are all fascinated by it. We want to understand it. But with due humility, we need to understand that there is a threshold of mystery. The journey of Light explains all other journeys. But itself? It is perhaps the ultimate mystery. 'Why' this journey in the first place? Well, because the Universe is here. But 'why' is it here? Well, because Light has been on its journey. We should not be too compulsive in trying to explain it all. Accepting mystery is actually rational. And it is beautiful. It adds profundity to the meaning of our lives.

CHAPTER 15

FOLLOW YOUR OWN NATURE

"While you live, shine."
— Epitaph of Seikilos
(circa 200 BC)

Follow your own nature... Your own deepest spiritual nature. Do not follow anybody else's nature. There are thousands of different flowers. Each blossoms differently. You have the right to blossom your own way.

We are all nourished by the same wonderful Mother Earth. We are all caressed by the same splendid sun. But the radiance of the sun is received and transformed in so many different ways. The spiritual light also can be received and transformed in so many different ways.

Find your own path. This path may already have a name. It may be called Taoist, Christian, Buddhist, Hindu, Muslim, Bahai. The name of the path is not important. Each of these paths is made of the eternal light of the universe—as received and transformed by various sages.

You are your own sage. You have the right to bask in the wisdom of the past. This is a gift of the universe given to each of us. You have the right to benefit from the enlightenment of past sages. They would be only too pleased if you do so.

Yet all the past enlightenment and all the past wisdom is but a reflection of the enormous light of the universe. You are part of the light of the universe. Shine your own light. The universe has made you in order that you can do so. For you are a ray of light of the universe.

Do not be afraid of your own light. Do not be afraid of yourself. This is a time to acknowledge that you are here to shine with the universe. If you are here not for this purpose, what purpose are you here for? You don't need to be arrogant about your own light. To acknowledge your own light is to acknowledge that the sun has blessed us all and that the universe is one miracle of light.

You are a small speck in the universe. But the Light of the universe is within you. You need to transform this light according to your own nature. And then shine with your own light.

CPSIA information can be obtained
at www.ICGtesting.com
Printed in the USA
LVHW081002131222
735126LV00026B/620

9 781734 804232